eWitness

Share your faith with
daily inspirational
Facebook posts and
Twitter tweets

*A*dvantage™
INSPIRATIONAL

Karen Stone-Janiczek, D.SL

eWitness by Karen Stone-Janiczek, D. SL.
Copyright © 2011 by Karen Stone-Janiczek
All Rights Reserved.
ISBN13: 978-1-59755-272-1

Published by: ADVANTAGE BOOKS™
www.advbookstore.com

Unless otherwise indicated, Bible quotations are taken from the Holy Bible, King James Version (KJV), public domain.

Library of Congress Control Number: 2011910585

Cover design by Pat Theriault

First Printing: July 2011
11 12 13 14 15 16 17   10 9 8 7 6 5 4 3 2 1
Printed in the United States of America

I dedicate this book to all of my facebook and twitter friends who encourage me to keep writing daily posts. Without your encouragement, I probably would have stopped writing them long ago and therefore, this book would not be.

To my parents Bernie and Mitzi Stone who taught me my morals.

To my sisters, Paula, Pamela, Tracy and Laura, we are all different and unique, and that is what makes us a family!

To my children Tiffany, Heather and David and his wife Leah who I love. God has great things for you.

To my husband Michael who inspires me everyday, you are my hero. Thank you for loving me for over 35 years. And for telling me to write this book.

And most of all to God who I love. To Jesus who saved me. And to the Holy Spirit who inspires and directs me everyday.

Karen Stone Janiczek

Endorsements

In March of 2011, I got lucky when a childhood friend, Karen Janiczek found me on Facebook. I was not surprised to find out that she had become an ordained Minister, knowing how kind and sweet she was as a teenager. Since that time, I have followed her postings on Facebook, passing on the Word of God. She has an incredible ability to explain what is written in the Bible that not only grabs my attention, but also gives me a great start to my day and inspires me to be a better person in my daily life. Now, when I get up in the morning, the first thing I do is to see what jewel Karen has posted for that day. She has been a driving force in helping me continue following Gods word.

Gregg England, Childhoof friend
Portland, Oregon

eWitness is a testament of the growing power of social media. Through social media any person's voice can instantly become global. Karen uses social media to inspire and give hope to her friends, followers, and readers. Karen's writing style is simple, enlightening, and motivational. eWitness will encourage you and empower you to live your faith every day one step at a time.

Ryan La Strange, Pastor, Impact International Ministries
Ryan LeStrange Ministries   P.O.Box16206 Bristol,VA24209
impactinternationalchurch.com, ryanlestrange.com

Karen Stone Janiczek

Forword

I am not a movie star or some other famous person, nor am I in politics or television. However, as a Christian I am a child of the King!

People call me "the blessed lady!" Am I blessed? Yes I am! They call me that because about 3 years ago I started to say I am blessed. When someone would say, Karen, How are you? I would say "blessed!" That's right, instead of saying fine, or good, or having a bad day, I would answer "blessed."

People would look at me strangely. Even Christians would say WHAT? Try saying that to your grocery clerk when checking out! You will be amazed at the responces. Usually they respond: "What?" And then I   say it again, "I am blessed."

I did that for about 6 months then I kicked it up a notch and said "I am greatly blessed!" Six months later, "I am greatly blessed and highly favored!" Yea I still get the looks and the whats! But many times people will say, "Me too!"

Now my daily confession is: I am greatly blessed and highly favored. Full of the annointing! Anything I put my hands to shall prosper. I walk in the fullness of God's plan for my life!

I am a wife and stay at home mom and raised my children. I believe that is the highest calling any woman can do. Now I am still a wife and mother, but I am also a business owner.

But that does not defind who I am. I am first and formost a child of the King. I daily, moment by moment, try to be led by the Holy Spirit. For over 3 years or so I would sit down at my desk and ask the Holy Spirit what would you have me post? That is what this book is about. It is my daily posts to my facebook friends.

I have had all kinds of responces. My friends tell me that they make a difference in their lives and they look for them daily.

They are set up in catagories but many can be used in several situations. Pray daily before you choose one to use. Ask God what do you want me to say today? He will guide and direct you daily You can make a difference in your cirlce of friends. I find that you only need to post one a day. If you post too many in a day you become annoying.

If I (no one famous) can inspire people so can you. You don't have to do something big, you just have to let God be in your life.

I hope they inspire you and lift you up. You can become my friend if you like on FACEBOOK (karenstone-janiczek) or TWITTER (@blessedkaryn) Be blessed!

Karen Stone-Janiczek

Table of Contents

What is eWitnessing ?

Simply put, eWitnessing is the door-to-door neighborhood ministry of the 21st Century

We now live in a world where kids and adults play football, basketball and hockey, but for most, it is in the simulated world of video games rather than outdoor sports. Most every kid in school has a cell phone and if you need any help with your computer, camera, video camera, Wii, X Box, I pad, nook, or kindle just ask your children or grandchildren.

Long gone are the lazy days when I was growing up in the 1960's. Kids now days could not imagine that we did not have cable TV and we actually had to get up and change the TV channels because there were no remote controls!

I remember in the seventies when we had the first "high tech" gadget of our day. It was a calculator that would add, subtract, multiply and divide. It was about the size of a 400 page book (5"wide X 8" tall X 2" thick). Its cost was $45.

The first video game I saw was pong, which was a black and white screen where you played ping-pong by moving the paddle (which was a white line that you could control moving up or down only) on your side of the screen to intersect and hit the ball (a little white dot that moved back and forth across your TV screen) before it went off your side of the screen.

We thought those things were really high tech! It was a big box about the size of a toolbox, with two round knobs that were your controllers that you wired to your TV. I think it cost about $50. Times have certainly changed!

When I was growing up and living in the south suburbs of Chicago, we personally knew everyone of the neighbors on our block, the block on either side of us. In addition, we pretty much knew the names of most everyone who lived within a mile or so of our house because if they had kids, we went to school with them.

I made lots of friends in those days but as life went on I lost touch with most of them. However because of computers, emails, the internet and social networks like **Facebook** or **Twitter**, we can now communicate with people more frequently and easier than ever before. In fact, we can now find long lost neighbors, classmates, family and friends around the world on the computer or using cell phone apps anytime and anywhere. I might never have spoken to some of these people again in my life, had not been for this technology.

When I first got on **Facebook**, I thought here is a medium that I could contact my family and friends from time to time. However, one day I sat at the computer on **Facebook** and suddenly I was inspired to post something about God. The response from my **Facebook** friends was overwhelming. So I decided to post something inspirational every day.

I have received so many messages since then from my friends telling me that they look for my posts every day and that the posts help them get through their days. Some have said that the posts were actually what they needed to hear that day.

That is when I realized that this form of daily messaging was a witness to my friends. I then coined the phrase "eWitness" to describe what I was doing.

This book is the accumulation of the inspirational posts and tweets that I sent out on **Facebook** and **Twitter** over the past few years. I have found this to be an incredible way for me to stay in contact with and share my faith on a daily basis with family and friends.

By using all or parts of these on your own posts or tweets, you too can inspire your **Facebook** and **Twitter** friends and make a difference for God.

Karen Stone Janiczek

How to get started

Join Facebook **at <u>www.facebook.com</u>**

Join Twitter **at <u>www.twitter.com</u>**

Search for family and/or friends by name.

Ask those friends if you can become their **Facebook** or **Twitter** friend. If they accept you as a **Facebook** and/or **Twitter** friend, you can communicate with them either privately or in public on your "wall" so that every one of your friends can see what you write.

Writing a public message on your wall in **Facebook** is called a "post". The guidelines of a post is that they can be up to but not exceeding 421 characters (including spaces).

Writing a public message in **Twitter** is called a "tweet". The guidelines of a tweet is that they can be up to but not exceeding 140 characters (including spaces).

The formats of my posts and tweets have already been designed to meet the character guidelines of **Facebook** posts and **Twitter** tweets.

Karen Stone Janiczek

POSTS and TWEETS

This is a list of the daily posts and tweets I used over the past two or three years on **Facebook** and **Twitter**. I have put them in categories for ease of use.

As I stated earlier, the unique quality of these inspirational thoughts are that posts are limited to 440 characters (including spaces) and tweets are limited to 140 characters (including spaces).

For the purposes of separation, the font of the posts appear in this book as regular type and the fonts of the tweets in this book are in *italics.*

Some original posts are shorter than 140 characters, therefore they can be used as both posts and tweets. They are at the back of each section and the font of these post/tweets is in ***bold italics***.

Some original posts required more than one tweet to convey the same idea. These can be sent one after the other to keep with the maximum character rule of tweets.

Karen Stone Janiczek

Section One

GOD'S GOODNESS

It is never too late to turn around and stop the bad behavior. God is a forgiving God and He wants us to succeed in life. You just have to say, "NO MORE!" Then ask God to help you. "With mans help I can attack an army. With God's help I can jump over a wall." Psalm 18:28-30

Stop bad behavior. God's 4giving. Say NO MORE! "With mans help I can attack an army. With God's help I can jump over a wall." Ps18:28-30

******

There is nothing that can separate you from God. His grace is sufficient for me. Do not walk in the law but walk in His grace. My God shall supply all of my needs according to His riches in Glory, by Christ Jesus.

There is nothing that can separate you from God. His grace is sufficient for me. Do not walk in the law but walk in His grace.

My God shall supply all of my needs according to His riches in Glory, by Christ Jesus.

******

I can't believe how good God is. He is blessing us beyond measure! Thank you Lord for all you have done and all you are going to do! I just praise your name!

God is good. He is blessing us beyond measure! Thank you Lord for all you have done and all you are going to do! I just praise your name!

******

Another great day! The weather is perfect! God is blessing us everyday! ISA 32:7 And the work of righteousness shall be peace; and the effect of righteousness quietness and assurance forever!

Another great day! God is blessing. ISA 32:7 the work of righteousness shall be peace the effect of righteousness quietness!

******

What a beautiful day it is today. The sun is shining. God loves you no matter what! Does not matter what you have done! Reach out to Jesus. He is the way the truth and the light.

What a beautiful day. God loves U & it does not matter what U have done! Reach out to Jesus. He is the way the truth the light.

******

People can lead to frustration. God will lead to peace. People will aggravate you. God will comfort you. People will yell at you. God talks in a small calm voice. People can hate. God only loves.

People can frustrate God is peace. People aggravate God comforts. People yell God talks in a calm voice. People hate, God loves.

######

Today I just want to say thank you Jesus! The same spirit that raised Christ from the dead dwells in me! What more do I need? I can do anything with that kind of power! Holy Spirit lead guide and direct my day. I just want to say I love you Lord and nothing can separate me from you!

2day I just want 2say thank U Jesus! Same spirit that raised Christ from the dead dwells N me What more do I need w power like that

######

There is nothing that can separate you from God. His grace is sufficient for me. Do not walk in the law but walk in His grace. My God shall supply all of my needs according to His riches in Glory, by Christ Jesus.

There is nothing that can separate you from God. His grace is sufficient for me. Do not walk in the law but walk in His grace.

My God shall supply all of my needs according to His riches in Glory, by Christ Jesus.

God is love. God loves us know matter what we have done. He will take you as you are...baggage and everything...and He won't charge extra for that!

God loves us know matter what we have done. He will take U as U R baggage & everything...He won't charge extra for that!

When you are at the end of your rope...God is there for you. When you are in the middle of your rope...God is there. When you are at the top of your rope...God is there. God loves you just the way you are.

Where R U on the rope? Beginning middle end? No matter where God is there 4 U!

******

God I praise your Holy name. You are awesome in all things. Thanks for blessing us this week. I am overwhelmed with your goodness. I will praise you in all things.

God I praise your Holy name. U R awesome Thanks 4 blessing us this week. I am overwhelmed with your goodness. I will praise U in all things.

******

God is with us all the time. He never leaves. He rejoices over us. Are you living a life that God would rejoice over? He loves us no matter what. He just hates the sin!

God with us & never leaves He rejoices over us R U living life that God would rejoice over? He loves us no matter what just hates the sin

******

God is good all the time. He never fails. He is there even when we are not. People think that God leaves us but we are the ones who walk away from Him. The cares of the world cause us to take our eyes off of Jesus. Stay focused by reading the Word daily and praying. Don't be on the defense but be on the offense. Pursue God daily. He wants to hear from you!

God is good always. He never fails He is there even when we R not. People think that God leaves us but we R the ones who walk away from Him

The cares of world cause us 2 take our eyes off Jesus Stay focused by reading the Word praying Don't B on defense but on offense Pursue God

******

Take time today to include God in your life. Start out small, 1 minute several times a day, talk to God. Pick up the Bible dust it off and read just 1 scripture verse today.

Take time 2 include God today. Start out small, 1 min several times a day, talk 2 God. Read the Bible just 1 scripture verse today.

******

God is number one in my life. In all things He is first. I go to Him first to ask Him what, where, when, why. When God is in control of your life, what more matters? Where does God stand in your life?

God is 1st in my life. Ask what, where, when, why? Gods in control, what more matters? Where does God stand in your life?

******

Reflect back...look forward. There is no rear view mirror with God. He has forgiven and He has forgotten your sin. So reflect back...but look forward!

Reflect back look forward. No rear view mirror with God. He has forgiven He has forgotten your sin. So reflect back...but look forward!

******

God is our strong tower, a fortress over me! That means God is unmovable, unstoppable and He covers me! I will abide in the tabernacle forever. I will trust in the covering of His wings. I will abide in His shadow. I put God first in all things. Where do you abide daily? Is God your strong tower?

God is our strong tower, a fortress over me! That means God is unmovable, & unstoppable & He covers me!

I will abide in the tabernacle forever. I will trust in the covering of His wings. I will abide in His shadow.

I put God first in all things. Where do you abide daily? Is God your strong tower?

******

God move in us. Thank you for all you have revealed to us. We only want what you want. Do not let us work in our own understanding but be led by You in all things.

God move. Thank you for revealing to us. Only want what You want. Do not let us work in our own understanding but be led by You.

******

God is so awesome! God talks to us all the time. God will talk and give you the answer or direction. Come on everyone...get quite with God and listen. You would be amazed how much He is talking to you!

God is so awesome! God talks to us all the time. God will talk and give us the answer direction.

Come on everyone...get quite with God and listen. You would be amazed how much He is talking to you!

Whenever you feel like giving up...instead of feeling down...look up! God is there to meet you wherever you are. He loves you so much and He wants to have fellowship with you. All you have to do is talk to Him.

When U feel like giving up look up! God is there. He loves you so much He wants 2 have fellowship. All U have to do is talk 2 Him.

******

Even though it may be cloudy and gray outside, God is always with us. Remember his mercy's are new every morning. Still meditating on that scripture.

Even though it may be cloudy & gray God is always with us. Remember His mercy's are new every morning.

******

When Noah built the ARK! He did not look at rain as a blessing. So much rain! No seriously, look at rain as a blessing that is coming your way. God is so good all the time.

Noah built the ARK he did not look at rain as blessing. So much rain! Look at rain as a blessing that is coming your way. God is so good all the time.

******

Today I am the righteousness of God through Christ Jesus. I am greatly blessed, highly favored, full of the anointing and anything I put my hand to will prosper!

I am the righteousness of God thru Christ. I am greatly blessed highly favored full of the anointing anything I put my hand to will prosper!

******

Going through this life so far I have learned that you try and you fail...you try again and fail....but the only true failure is when you stop trying. With God all things are possible.

U try/U fail, U try again/U fail again, the only 1 true failure is when U stop trying. With God all things R possible.

******

God is so good all the time. If God is for us then who can be against us. Is there anything our God cannot do? You just have to ASK: ask seek knock.

God is good always. If God is for us then who can be against us. Is there anything our God cannot do? You just have to ASK: ask seek knock.

******

God is in control of all things. No matter what the circumstances are. I will keep my eyes on Jesus and I know that He will be victorious in all things! No weapon formed against me shall prosper! Call those things that be not as though they were!

God is in control of all. No matter the circumstances. I will keep my eyes on Jesus and I know that He will be victorious in all things!

No weapon formed against me shall prosper! Call those things that be not as though they were!

******

God is good and faithful all the time. I am rejoicing today for His goodness! When one prays expect answers! God is in the answering prayer business. Try it and see!

God is faithful. Expect when U pray! God is in the business of answering prayers. Try it and see!

Do you hear the voice of God? Does He speak to you? God is speaking to all of us daily, but if you are not hearing Him, then you are not listening. Maybe you don't know what the Voice of God sounds like. Maybe you're not tuned in. Shut everything off, dig into the Word and start talking to Him. Conversation is a two way street. Maybe just maybe, you are not talking to God.

Do you hear the voice of God? Does He speak to you? God is speaking to all, but if you're not hearing Him, then you are not listening.

R U tuned in? Do U know the Voice of God? Turn everything off, dig into the Word & start talking to Him conversation a two way street.

******

Everyday God is love. Everyday God is merciful. Everyday God is good. Everyday God is there. Everyday God is blessing. Everyday God is talking. Where are you everyday?

Everyday God is love & merciful. Everyday He is good & is there. Everyday God is blessing. Everyday God is talking. Where are you everyday?

Good morning...good morning...what a great day! Sun is shinning and God is on the throne! Jesus lives in my heart and I have the Holy Spirit working with me! What more do I need? I am so blessed!

What a great day sun is shinning God is on the throne! Jesus lives in my heart I have the Holy Spirit working with me! What more do I need?

******

God is good even in the trouble times. Even though you may be walking through the valley, God is there. You just have to reach out and talk to Him. Lay your troubles at His feet and then start thanking Him for the answer. God comes through every time!

God is good in the trouble times. Though you may be walking through the valley God is there. You just have to reach out and talk to Him.

Lay your troubles at His feet and then start thanking Him for the answer. God comes through every time!

******

Let's see how many people on fb aren't ashamed to show their love for God and admit that Jesus is their Savior. We need to get God back in America. If you're not ashamed, copy and paste this in your status--- No Shame here!

How many people aren't ashamed 2 show their love 4 God & admit that Jesus is Lord. Get God back in America. Copy paste No Shame here!

******

Today I am blessed and highly favored by the Lord. Today I am standing on the promises of God. Today I will not look to the right or to the left; I will keep my eyes on Jesus. He is my strength in times of trouble. I will praise Him in the good times and in the bad times. Where do you find your strength?

Today I am blessed and highly favored by the Lord. Today I am standing on the promises of God.

Today I will not look to the right or left, I will keep my eyes on Jesus.

He is my strength in times of trouble. I will praise Him in the good times and in the bad times. Where do you find your strength?

******

Everyday God is doing great things in our lives. Even when we think He has left us. He does not change...we do. Reach out to Him today. He wants to be your solution. Give everything over to Him, you won't go wrong. Remember you are blessed and highly favored.

Everyday God is doing great things in our lives. Even when we think He has left us. He does not change. We do.

Reach out to Him today. He wants to be your solution. Give everything over to Him U won't go wrong. Remember U R blessed & highly favored.

******

This is the day the Lord hath made, I will rejoice and be glad in it. Putting God first is the only way. Why do it on your own? God wants to take control. Just let Him.

This is the day the Lord hath made, I will rejoice and be glad in it.
Putting God first is the only way. Why do it on your own? God wants to take control. Just let Him.

******

Even when we are playing and resting, God is still in control. We want to be led by the Holy Spirit in all things. Not sometimes Holy Spirit...but ALL times Holy Spirit! I am ALL IN! Are you?

At play & rest Gods in control. B led by Holy Spirit in all things Not sometimes Holy Spirit but ALL times Holy Spirit! I am ALL IN Are you?

******

When God moves He Moves! The Power of God is so strong and sometimes you can not take it! I thank you Lord for your words. I will bless your name forever more.

When God moves He Moves! Power of God is strong & sometimes U can not take it thank you Lord 4 your word. I will bless your name 4ever more.

******

What is your relationship with God? Do you talk to Him everyday? Or does your words only include God when you are mad? He wants a relationship with you. Just take time to talk to Him.

What is your relationship with God? Do you talk to Him everyday? Or does your words only include God when you are mad?

He wants a relationship with you. Just take time to talk to Him.

******

I am blessed...I am blessed...I am blessed and highly favored...why? Because of all that God has done for me. And God loves me no matter what. Oh did I say I am blessed?

I am blessed I am blessed & highly favored why? Because all God has done for me. And God loves me no matter what. Oh did I say I am blessed?

Tweets And Posts
(These Can Be Used For Both)

The sun is shining today, God is on the throne and we are blessed! Life is expanding and prospering. We are greatly blessed and highly favored!

******

Sunday Christian? Or Everyday Christian?

******

What is God telling you? Are you listening?

******

What is your spiritual DNA?

******

I am blessed even when I'm not!

******

Are you GBHF today? Greatly blessed highly favored!

******

No better place to be than at church after a long day! Spending time with the Lord...priceless!

******

Are you comfortable in your discomfort? Think about it!

******

God comes through every time!

******

Praise God...prayer works!

******

Sometimes you forget how important your prayer language is in your life. That is where the power is!
God is good...God is good...God is good!!

******

So tired...Lord thank you for being busy. Thank you for your blessings.

******

God is God all the time. Do you rely on Him all the time? If not, what are you relying on?

******

Take time today to reflect on what God has done for you. Then praise and thank Him for His wondrous Glory. God is good all the time.

******

Thank you Lord for moving this morning. Lives have been changed. And thank you God for using us. Move and guide and direct us.

******

It is good to remember our Christian roots. God is not finished with us yet! The best is yet to come!

******

Do you have the heart of God for His people? I humbly go before you seeking your face in all things.

******

God is good all the time. No matter what. No matter where, No matter when. God is good all the time!

******

When God shows up...He shows up BIG! You just may not be hearing Him!

******

This is the day that the Lord has made. I will rejoice and be glad in it!

******

Enjoying what God has to give to me!
Working at my desk, enjoying the goodness of God.

******

Trusting in God in all things. What more do you need.

******

Today God told me to be silent and know that He is God.

******

Thank you Lord for your love and grace for me.

******

Living for God! Can't do any better than that.

******

God is so good. I am starting to hear Him more, and when I do I am acting on what He is telling me.

******

Enjoying this beautiful spring day. God is so good.

******

Finding God's favor in my life!

******

Resting in God's favor!

******

Believe with me...need answer to my prayer. Restoration

******

Who are you serving today?

******

I am blessed and highly favored therefore I am the righteousness of God in Christ Jesus.

******

All I can say is God is so good! He comes through every time! Thank you God for all you do in our lives!

******

The Lord is my God, my rock, my strength, my deliverer, my healer, my provider, my comforter in whom I trust! What more do I need?

There is nothing that can separate U from God. His grace is sufficient 4 me. Do not walk in the law but walk in His grace.

******

My God shall supply all of my needs according to His riches in Glory, by Christ Jesus.

******

Section Two

BORN AGAIN

You never know when you are going to die so make sure that you know Jesus in a personal way. John 3:16 I can't even imagine how long eternity is.

U never know when U R going 2 die make sure that U know Jesus in a personal way. John 3:16 I can't even imagine how long eternity is.

******

Do you know that when you become born again you became new? That means your old self is dead. That God who created the heavens and the earth has made you new. Don't look to your past, don't say, "Well I have always been like that!" Don't blame your parents for how you are. You are now a NEW creation of God. All things have past away and you are brand new. Clean slate. With God all things are possible.

Do U know that when U become born again U became new? Your old self is dead. God who created the heavens and the earth has made you new.

Don't look to your past, "Well I have always been like that!" Don't blame your parents for how U R. U R now a NEW creation of God.

All things have past away & U R brand new. Clean slate. With God all things R possible.

******

When facing surgery people start to think of where will I go when I die? If you know Jesus as your personal Savior then you know. But if you don't know Him in a personal way...why? Salvation is for everyone. You choose. Where would you like to spend eternity?

Facing surgery we start to think of where will go when we die? If you know Jesus as your personal Savior then you know.

But if you don't know Him in a personal way...why? Salvation is for everyone. You choose. Where would you like to spend eternity?

******

Have you ever looked into your heritage? Where did we come from? Who were are ancestors? It made me think, we all come from somewhere/someone. But the great part of salvation that God gave us is for all. God sent His son, Jesus, to die for all of us. To save us from our sins no matter who we are or where we came from.

Who do you think you are? Our Biblical heritage is great. Abraham, Isaac, Jacob, great men of faith who set a great example for us all.

******

God loves you...God loves you...God loves you...God loves you...God loves you...Did I mention that God loves you...no matter what! Nothing you have done can make God not love you. He loves you but hates the sin. Turn to Jesus for your salvation.

God loves you...God loves you...God loves you...God loves you...God loves you...Did I mention that God loves you...no matter what!

Nothing you have done can make God not love you. He loves you but hates the sin. Turn to Jesus for your salvation.

******

Ever watch Fiddler on the Roof. It makes me glad that I am saved by grace and don't work in the law. Jesus died for us to abolish the law. The law was only given to revel sin. Just like Yom Kippur, Jesus was the sacrifice and He paid forward for forgiveness of our sins. Read Romans 7 & 8 and live in grace.

Ever watch Fiddler on the Roof. It makes me glad that I am saved by grace & not in the law. Jesus died 4 us to abolish the law.

The law was only given to revel sin. Just like Yom Kippur, Jesus was the sacrifice and He paid forward for forgiveness of our sins. Romans 7 & 8 live in grace.

******

It doesn't matter what the President says, or what congress does, or if the senate passes this bill or that, or who is in the government. What does matter is do you know Jesus as your personal Savior? When we die we either go to heaven or hell. Now that matters!!

Doesn't matter what President says congress senate pass a bill? What matters do U know Jesus? We die we go 2 heaven or hell Now that matters!

******

Today is a great day in Christ. God is on the throne and Jesus reigns forever. What more can you ask for? Jesus is the Lord of my life. John 3:16 Who so ever calls on the name of the Lord shall be saved. Have you made Him Lord in your life?

God on the throne Jesus reigns Lord of my life. John 3:16 Who ever calls on name Lord shall be saved. Have you made Him Lord in your life?

******

The Bible says that it is once appointed to man to die, and then judgment. Which master do you serve? Jesus is the way the truth and the life and with Him you will have eternal life. To live forever with Jesus in heaven. But you have to ask Him into your heart and life. Where are you going when you die?

Bible says that it is once appointed to man to die, and then judgment. Which master do you serve?

Jesus the way truth & life with Him eternal life 2 live forever with Jesus in heaven U ask Him into your heart. Where R U going when U die?

******

When someone is on their deathbed, it makes you think...how precious life is and where are you going when you die? If you don't know then you may want to think about it. Jesus is the only way to heaven. John 3:16 Look it up and find the truth and the truth will set you free. Be blessed!

Someone is on their deathbed, it makes you think, how precious life is & where R U going when U die? Don't know then think about it.

Jesus is the only way to heaven. John 3:16 find the truth & the truth will set you free. Be blessed!
******

Can you think of a time that you needed God? Did you reach out and call on Him? He is there all the time, in the good and in the bad. You just have to cry out to Him and He will answer.

Can U think of time that U need God? Did U call on Him? He is there always in the good and in the bad U have to cry out 2 Him He will answer.
******

Mercy is not getting something that you deserve. Grace is more than mercy. Mercy gets a criminal off the hook and out of jail....but grace pays the debt of the criminal and sets him free. Jesus paid our debt and set us free.

Mercy gets a criminal off, Grace pays the debt & sets him free. Jesus paid our debt and set us free.
******

Jacob in the Bible really messed up, and still God blessed him! When we mess up we think God does not love us or we can't be blessed by Him. WRONG!!! Sin does not matter! Jesus' blood washed away our sins, when we ask Him into our hearts! It is Finished! Those are Jesus words!

Jacob N Bible messed up God blessed him! We mess up think God does not love us can't be blessed, WRONG!

WRONG! Sin does not matter Jesus blood washed away our sins, when we ask Him into R heart It is Finished! Jesus words!

******

The way to God is not by works but by His grace and through His son Jesus. John 3:16 Believe in your heart that Jesus is Lord and ask Him to come into your life today. So simple!

Way 2 God is not by works but by His grace & thru Jesus. John 3:16 Believe Jesus is Lord ask Him 2 come in2 your life So simple!

******

Turmoil is all over the world. You never know what will happen in your life. Make Jesus Lord of your life and be sure of eternal life. Have peace and assurance in Him. Jesus loves you no matter what. Just ask Him into your life today.

Turmoil in world Never know what will happen Make Jesus Lord B sure of eternal life. Peace assurance in Him. Jesus loves you. Ask Him.

******

God is not complicated! God sent His son Jesus to die for our sins! All we have to do is accept that! God loves us so much He made a way to have fellowship with Him. It is us who make it so complex! Ask Jesus to be the Lord of your life today, don't wait!

God is not complicated! God sent His son Jesus to die 4 our sins! All we have to do is accept that!

God loves us He made a way 2 have fellowship. We make it complex! Ask Jesus 2 B Lord of your life 2day, don't wait!

Kingdoms come and kingdoms go. Kingdoms rise and kingdoms fall. The only Kingdom that will stand the test of time is the Kingdom of God. It was, it is, and it will be to come. Come into the Kingdom of God today. Don't wait!

Kingdoms come/go rise/fall. Stand test of time Kingdom of God. It was, it is,it will be to come. Come into the Kingdom of God today. Don't wait!

******

Choices! Right or wrong choices! You weave through life meeting people and leaving people. Along the way you grow by the choices and people you meet. Have you met Jesus along your journey? Have you made the choice to ask Jesus into your life and make him first in your life? Remember no one will love you like the love of God.

U make choices & U meet people thru life meeting people. Have U met Jesus along your journey?

Have you made the choice to ask Jesus into your life & make him first in your life? Remember no one will love U like the love of God.

******

Today could be the last day of your life. When you are young we think we have all the time in the world for God. When we are middle age we can't seem to find the time for God. When we are old we start thinking about is there a God. Why wait till you are old? God is now, God is real, God is here! Ask Jesus into your life. Make Him Lord of your life. Now! Not later!

When U R young we think we have lots of time 4 God. Middle Age: too busy. Old Age: start thinking about God Why wait till U R old. Do it 2day

******

The very best athletics give their very best. Should we as Christians give our very best every day? The athletics represent their countries. We Christians represent God. Gold is the ultimate reward for the Olympics. Jesus is our reward. Surrender your heart to Him and reap His rewards.

Athletics represent their country Christians represent God. Athletics train Christians read the word. Give your very best 2 God

Tweets And Posts
(These Can Be Used For Both)

Think of the things He's saved us from that we thought were good decisions or the "wants" of the moment.

Section Three

FAITH

What can you do? He can move mountains! He wants to bless us! He is our strength/strong tower! EPH 3:20 Now to Him who is able to do exceedingly abundantly above all that we ask or think, according to the power that works in us. I can think pretty big! Seek Him first & all these things shall be added unto you. Do you seek Him daily? Is He first all the time? What is God calling you to do? Ask Seek Knock!

He can move mountains EPH 3:20 2 Him who is able 2 do exceedingly abundantly above all we ask/think, according 2 power that works in us.

I can think pretty big! Seek Him 1ˢᵗ all things shall be added 2 you. Do you seek Him? Is He first? What is God calling you to do? Ask Seek Knock

******

Do you believe in the Bible? If so then you should believe in the whole Bible...right? Or are you one to pick and choose what to believe? Or are you one to believe your own way. We all are different, but one thing for sure that's in the Bible, God loves us no matter what! I like that! Be blessed!

Do U believe in the Bible? Should U believe in the whole Bible? R U 1 2 pick /choose what 2 believe? U believe your own way?

We all R different but 1 thing 4 sure in the Bible it says God loves us no matter what! I like that! Be blessed!

******

What do other people believe & why? Glad that I know the Risen Savior and God the Father. Glad that I know He loves me & I am saved. Glad to know that no matter what God is there for me. Glad to know that He will never let me down. Like I said before I am all in and I am GBHF!

What do other people believe & why? Glad that I know the Risen Savior & God the Father. Glad that I know that He loves me & that I am saved.

Glad 2 know no matter what God is there 4 me. Glad 2 know that He will never let me down. Like I said before I am all in and I am GBHF!

******

You know just when you are at your ropes end. God shows up! Shows up BIG! Never, I mean never doubt what God can do in your life! Have...Now Faith...for things you need. Thank you God for providing for us in all things!

Ropes end? God will show up! Never doubt, have faith. God will provide.

******

Sometimes it is hard to remember that Jesus heals. My symptoms scream ear infection, soar throat, headache, but the Word says, By Jesus stripes I am healed. I am taking meds, and I am trusting God that I am healing fast. I am healed in Jesus name!

Jesus heals. My symptoms scream at me but Word says, By Jesus stripes I am healed. I am healed in Jesus name!

******

God is good all the time...let me say that again...God is good all the time. No matter what you are going through. Don't give up. Keep pressing through. Stand on scripture. Call those things that be not as though they were. Speak it! Faith is speaking it out loud until it comes. Rest in God's love while you are going through it.

God is good all the time No matter U R going thru. Don't give up. Keep pressing through. Stand on scripture.

Call those things that be not as tho they were. Speak it Faith speak out loud until it comes. Rest in God's love while U R going through it.

******

Speak it forth! The Bible says call those things that be not as tho they were. What do you want? What is God telling you to do? Now faith is the substance of things hoped for the evidence of things not seen. So, your faith, is calling those things that be not as tho they were. Speak out loud to God what you are believing for. Don't think it or whisper it in a weak prayer. Go boldly before the Lord, speak it forth!

Speak it forth! The Bible says call those things that be not as tho they were. What do you want? What is God telling you to do?

Now faith is the substance of things hoped 4 evidence of things not seen. Your faith is calling those things that be not as tho they were.

Speak out loud to God what you are believing for. Don't think it or whisper it in a weak prayer. Go boldly before the Lord, speak it forth!

******

Okay, here is our confession this week: I am greatly blessed, highly favored, full of the anointing, anything I put my hand to will prosper, and I am living in the fullness of God's plan for my life. Enough Said!

I am blessed highly favor full of the anointing anything I put my hand to will prosper I am living in the fullness of God's plan for my life.

******

Amazing Jesus died like all of us will do one day. But the Holy Spirit came and raise Him from death. If you believe in God and in Jesus then, "That same spirit that raised Christ from the dead dwells in me." That is pretty powerful! "I am joint Heirs with Jesus." "A child of the King!" What can I not do?

Jesus died like we do, but the Holy Spirit raised Him from the dead. That same spirit that raised Christ from the dead dwells in me.

******

Your faith can move mountains. Your faith like a grain of mustard seed can change your situation. When things start to move sometimes we are amazed. Hear the voice of God, then implement what He is telling you things start to happen! I am GBHF, full of the anointing and anything I put my hand to will prosper!

Your faith can move mountains. Your faith like a grain of mustard seed can change your situation.

When things start to move sometimes we are amazed. Hear the voice of God, then implement what He is telling you things start to happen!

******

Just thinking about how good God is. Many people do not feel that way. Why? Circumstances, they are far from or mad at God. They have unbelief. They want God to make it better. Like a Band-Aid, but God is not a Band-Aid He is better. God wants to be part of our lives. He wants daily interaction. He wants to be your everything. Ask Jesus into your life today.

Thinking about how good God is. People do not feel that way Why? Circumstances, they are far from or mad at God. They have unbelief.

God is not a Band-Aid He is better. Make Him part of life & daily interaction. Ask Jesus in2 your life today.

******

Without faith it is impossible to please God. If you are going through something or are waiting for an answer you need to proclaim your faith. Call those things that be not as though they were. Call what you need into being. Faith is the answer!

Without faith it is impossible to please God. Going through something? Faith is the answer!

******

Should I give up? Should I not try? Could I say, "This is too hard!" NO! I should not give up! Yes it is hard, but my God is bigger and greater than anything! When you are at your wits end, ask God for a gift of FAITH! Faith is what you need to get your through the storm. Faith is what you need to keep trying. Faith and God.

Should I give up not try? "This is too hard!" NO! I should not give up! Yes it is hard, but my God is bigger and greater than anything!

When U are at your wits end ask God 4 a gift of FAITH! Faith what U need 2 get you thru the storm & 2 keep trying. Faith & God.

******

Today if you are feeling down...look up! Talk to God about your troubles. Tell Him, even thou He knows what you are going through. He likes to have fellowship with us. That is why He created us. So sit down today and talk to God. He wants to answer your prayers. Start activating your faith! Declare that you are blessed and highly favored! Declare that you are prosperous!

Today feeling down look up! Talk 2 God about your troubles. Tell Him He likes 2 have fellowship with us. That is why He created us.

Talk 2 God. He wants 2 answer prayers. Start activating your faith! Declare that U R blessed highly favored! Declare that U R prosperous!

What do you need? Nothing is impossible for God! Yes you may grow weary but faith without works is dead! The Joy of the Lord is our strength! Keep pressing on with God and see what the Lord will do for you!

What do U need? Nothing is impossible 4 God! U may grow weary but faith without works is dead!

The Joy of the Lord is our strength! Keep pressing on with God and see what the Lord will do for you!

******

God is good all the time, no matter what! Don't look to the right or left, but keep your eyes on Jesus. Don't give up. Keep pressing forward in faith.

God is good all the time no matter what! Don't look 2 the right/left keep your eyes on Jesus. Don't give up keep pressing 4ward in faith.

******

Ever hear that song with the lyrics "When God speaks His voice is thunder and lightning and shakes the foundations of the earth." With a God like that what more do we need? He has given us that same power Jesus had and with that power what can we not do? Faith is that power! Call upon His name in all things and have faith!

When God speaks His voice is thunder lightning shakes the foundations of the earth. With a God like that what more do we need?

He has given us that same power Jesus had with that power what can we not do? Faith=power! Call upon His name in all things & have faith!

Don't look at the circumstances, look to God. Give God your burdens and problems let Him work them out. Lean not to your own understanding. Remember that old song, Lean on me, well lean on God. Stand on faith and call those things that be not as though they were.

Don't look at circumstances, look 2 God. Give God your burdens let Him work them out. Lean not 2 your own understanding lean on God.

******

When God talks to you, do you listen? Sometimes when God talks to you, there may be doubt that you are hearing from Him. He wants you to act on what He is telling you. These times it takes faith to step out to do, say what He is telling you. When you step out in faith it can be scary but with God how can you loose. When things happen you know you heard from God. Seek, listen, do.

When God talks do U listen? Do U doubt? Takes faith 2 step out & do. Things happen U know U heard from God. Seek listen do.

******

First a light snow but as the day wears on a blizzard! This is much like our walk with God. We start out small in our prayers and bible reading. If we diligently seek Him we should daily grow in these areas. And as we grow so does our faith. Without faith it is impossible to please God. How much faith do you have? What are you believing for?

Light snow now blizzard! This is much like our walk with God. Start out small in prayer & bible reading & diligently seek Him=growth=faith.

Without faith it is impossible to please God. How much faith do you have? What are you believing for?
******

"He who creates a good work in me will be faithful to complete it." God is faithful to complete it so why do we work in our own understanding. God says, He is faithful and if God is going to complete it why would I want to do it? He can do much more than I ever could. I know God is not finished with me yet, so He is faithful to complete it in me. Stand back and see what God can complete.

He who creates a good work in me will be faithful 2 complete it. God is faithful 2 complete it. Why do we work in our own understanding?

He is faithful & if God completes it why would I want to do it? He can do much more than I ever could.

I know God is not finished with me yet, so He is faithful to complete it in me. Stand back and see what God can complete.
******

I will give thanks to God in all things. I know you are probably getting tired of hearing that but, I do. Especially in tough times. I am victorious in Christ Jesus.

I will give thanks to God in all things. Especially in tough times. I am victorious in Christ Jesus.
******

God tells you to do something, do it! God wants to see your faith for Him to make it happen. We are standing on God's word and see the wondrous hand of God bring it to past. Without faith it is impossible to please God. Where is your faith?

God tells you 2 do something do it! God wants 2 see your faith. Stand on God's word see the hand of God bring it 2 past. Where is your faith?

******

God is my provider in all things. I am expecting God to show up big in my life. I am standing on His promises. In all things! No matter what my situation is, no matter what anyone says. My God shall supply all of my needs in Christ Jesus.

God is my provider. Expecting God 2 show up big. Standing on His promises. No matter what My God shall supply all of my needs in Christ Jesus.

******

God is so good. I am joint heirs with Jesus. God will supply all my needs. Call those things as though they were! By Jesus stripes we were healed! What do you need? Go to God in all things! Give Him a chance and see what He can do!

God is good & will supply my needs Call those things as tho they were! By Jesus stripes we were healed! What do U need? See what He can do!

******

I am prosperous, I am healthy, I am healed, I am saved by grace, I am walking in the anointing, I am walking in the fullness of what Christ has for me, I am moving forward in the assurance and peace that God is in control of my life, and did I mention I am blessed and highly favored! Thought I would forget that one! Never!

I am prosperous healthy saved by grace. Walking in the anointing & the fullness of what Christ has 4 me.

I am moving forward in the assurance & peace that God is in control of my life, I am blessed highly favored!

******

Do you only go to God when things are getting tough? You need to go to Him when things are good too. You need to be grounded in prayer at all times, so when the tough times come...you can be strong in Him. Be pro-active in your prayer life. Read your Bible everyday and go to church. Three things to stay strong in the Lord. And remember...run from SIN!

Only go 2 God when things R tough? Need 2 go 2 Him when things R good. B grounded in prayer so when tough times come U can B strong in Him.

Be pro-active in your prayer life. Read your Bible everyday & go 2 church. 3 things to stay strong in the Lord. Remember, .run from SIN!

******

Getting presents makes you happy! Kids want their gifts NOW! But sometimes we have to wait. Getting something from God can be like that. We want it now, but God's timing may be to wait. When He answers there is always joy. Faith is what I use while I am waiting. I know I want what God has for me even if I have to wait.

We want it NOW! Sometimes we have 2 wait 4 God's time. While waiting I use Faith. I want what God has 4 me even if I have 2 wait.

******

God I praise your name today. I give you thanks in all you do. I will glorify your name above all names. Jesus you are our salvation and you are our healer. Without you I am nothing.

With God I can do all things. Nothing is impossible with God. I can soar on wings of eagles!

God I praise & thank you. I glorify your name above all names. Jesus U R our salvation & healer. Without you I am nothing.

With God I can do all things. Nothing is impossible with God. I can soar on wings of eagles!
******

How much of the Bible do you believe? Do you pick and choose like in a supermarket? I'll have salvation but not healing. Must be my lot in life, but not that faith thing! God gave many promises, we need to pull them down. Ask seek knock. May you prosper as your soul prospers. Ask what you will & it will be given to you. I want my storehouse in heaven to be empty. I want all that God has for me here.

How much of the Bible do U believe? Do U pick & choose like in a supermarket? Salvation yes healing no. My lot in life not that faith thing!

God gave many promises, we need to pull down on them. Ask seek knock. May you prosper as your soul prospers.

Ask what you will & it will be given to you. I want my storehouse in heaven 2 B empty. I want all that God has 4 me here.
******

Do you believe in the Bible? If so then you should believe in the whole Bible, right? Or are you one to pick and choose what to believe? Or are you one to believe your own way? We all are different, but 1 thing for sure it says in the Bible God loves us no matter what! I like that! Be blessed!

Believe in the Bible? The whole Bible? Do U pick & choose what U want 2 believe? 1 thing 4 sure God loves U!

******

Sometimes life is hard. Sometimes life is good. Sometimes life is sad, and sometimes glad. It is easy to Praise God in the good times, but what are you doing in the hard times? In everything give thanks. My Praise will continually be in my mouth.

Life is hard/good Sad/glad Easy 2 Praise God in good times what R U doing in hard times? In all give thanks Praise will always b in my mouth

Tweets And Posts
(These Can Be Used For Both)

Believe with me...need answer to your prayers. Restoration, Thank you Jesus!

******

Okay Go, .today I am expecting you to show up big! I am calling those things that be not as though they were. Now faith!

******

I am believing for total healing from God. By Jesus stripes I am healed. Amen! I am GBHF always!

******

God cares for us. That He is there in the midst of the storm. Thank you God for that blessing.

******

God loves us so much. Even in times of pain. Lean on Jesus through this time.   Everyday God is good. Still believing for miracles.

******

In everything give thanks. Don't feel like Praising but going to! In Jesus name I am healed! That's my confession I am sticking to it!

******

Sometimes you just have to plow through. Don't look at your circumstance Just keep your eyes on Jesus.

******

Bible says give thanks in ALL things. Sometimes that is hard.

******

Working and still waiting on God!

******

How can you please God? The Bible says, without faith it is impossible to please God. Heb 11:6 How are you pleasing God today?

******

Think like a person of action and act like a person of thought...that's how you keep the flesh under and are able to walk in love.

Section Four

BEING LED BY THE HOLY SPIRIT

Who are you listening to? If your answer is anything but the Holy Spirit you need to stop and evaluate. Don't do anything unless the Holy Spirit says to do it. If you don't know which way, just ask. He will tell you. But you need to listen. I know that I am listening.

Who R U listening 2? Need 2 stop & evaluate Move with the Holy Spirit Direction just ask He will tell U. Listen I know that I am listening.

******

What is your first reaction when something bad happens? Do you respond with your feelings? Lashing out in anger? That is usually our first responce. Try taking a deep breath and ask the Holy Spirit how to react. That is harder and not as easy to do but I suspect it will be the right responce.

What is your first reaction when something bad happens? Respond with your feelings? Lashing out in anger? That is usually our first responce.

Try taking a deep breath ask the Holy Spirit how 2 react. That is harder & not as easy 2 do but I suspect it will be the right responce.

******

Exhausting day! "He who dwells in the shadow of the Most High will abide in the shadow of the Almighty." I say to the Lord, "My refuge and my fortress, My God in whom I trust. For it is He who delivers you from the snare of the trapper." Psalm 91. Meditate on this Psalm. Listen to the Holy Spirit.

Exhausting day! "He who dwells in the shadow of the Most High will abide in the shadow of the Almighty."

I will say to the Lord, "My refuge and my fortress, My God in whom I trust. For it is He who delivers you from the snare of the trapper." Psalm 91

******

When war is over there are casualties! Walking away and not engaging is not the thing your flesh wants to do. Your flesh wants to engage, roar ahead, but walking away and being led by the Spirit you have the peace of God. For we wrestle not against flesh and blood, but against principalities, against powers and the rulers of the darkness of this world, against spiritual wickedness in high places. Eph6:12

War is over there R casualties! Walk away & not engage not the thing your flesh wants 2 do walk away B led by the Spirit have peace of God.

We wrestle not against flesh & blood but against principalities powers rulers of darkness against spiritual wickedness in high places Eph6:12

******

Sweet! What is sweet? I could say my life is sweet! Sweet because I have Jesus in my life. Sweet because I am following the Holy Spirit. I don't know why today I have been thinking about the word sweet? But I do know life would not be sweet without Jesus. How sweet is your life?

Sweet what is sweet? My life is sweet I have Jesus in my life I do know life would not be sweet without Jesus. How sweet is your life?

******

Have you ever had to turn the other cheek? Not once, but many times? It is hard to do that. Your flesh screams out, "XJFKXZG" not productive. What would Jesus do? You can't hear because your flesh is yelling so loud. We need to not react but listen to the HIS voice. Telling your flesh to lie down is hard, but listening to the HIM is productive.

Have you turn the other cheek? Hard 2 do your flesh screams out "XJFZ" not productive. Stop listen what would Jesus do?

U can't hear Him because your flesh is yelling We need not react/listen 2 HIM. Tell flesh 2 lie down:hard listening 2 the HIM:productive

******

Always be yourself, be real. Change is good, never be afraid to try something new. Remember amateurs built the ark and it survived the great storm. But professionals built the Titanic and it sank in the ocean. Don't ever feel inadequate you can do and be anything you want to be. You need to rely on the Lord for help.

Always B yourself B real. Change is good try something new. Amateurs built the Ark, professionals built the Titanic. Follow the leading of the Holy Spirit.

******

Sometimes you find yourself facing a GIANT wall! What should I do? Go left, go right, go over it? Our first reaction is to charge ahead, no matter what! Don't think just go! But what we need to do is sit back pray. Holy Spirit lead me, guide me, show me. That can be hard cause we have to wait listen, not charge ahead! Lord I am waiting...and listening!

Find yourself facing a GIANT wall! What should I do? 1st reaction charge no matter what! Don't think just go! Need 2 stop pray.

Holy Spirit lead me, guide me, show me. That can B hard we have 2 wait listen, not charge ahead! Lord I am waiting & listening!

******

Looking forward to what God has for us! Holy Spirit works in us. God I want to be what You want me to be. I live everyday putting you first! I am Greatly blessed and highly favored of the Lord!

Looking forward 2 what God has 4 me! God I want 2 B what U want me 2 B. I live everyday putting you first!

******

I am amazed at what God is doing in my life. Satan may try to throw things in my way, but powering through with God. Listening to the Holy Spirit. It's better to follow the Holy

Spirit. If we listen and do what the Holy Spirit is telling us to do, how can we fail? It's when we take things in our own hands that trouble follows.

Amazed what God's doing my life Satan try 2 throw things my way power thru w God. Listen 2 Him We take things in our own hands trouble follows.

******

When Jesus went into the wilderness he was full of the Holy Spirit, but when he came out he was operating in the Holy Spirit. My prayer is that I am operating in the Holy Spirit. My new confession, I am greatly blessed, highly favored and full of the anointing. Lord use me, guide me every day.

Jesus went into wilderness he was full of Holy Spirit he came out operating in Holy Spirit. My prayer is that I am operating in Holy Spirit.

My new confession, I am greatly blessed, highly favored and full of the anointing. Lord use me, guide me every day.

******

Where does God have you? Where do you fit in? If you don't know, ask God for direction for your life. Don't move without the Holy Spirit telling you to move. Use the talent that God has given you for His purpose.

Where does God have you? Do you fit in? Ask God 4 direction don't move without Him telling you. Use the talent God gave U 4 His purpose.

******

It is good to follow the Holy Spirit. Don't second-guess what Holy Spirit is telling you. Move forward in God. Move forward to what God has for you.

Karen Stone Janiczek

Good 2 follow Holy Spirit. Don't second-guess what Holy Spirit is telling you. Move forward in God. Move forward to what God has for you

******

When God talks...do you hear? When God speaks...do you listen? When God moves...do you receive? When God is there...do you know He is there? God is the Alpha, Omega, the beginning and the end. Where are you when God shows up?

When God talks do U hear? God speaks U listen? God moves U receive? God is there U know He is there?

God is the Alpha, Omega, the beginning and the end. Where are you when God shows up?

******

God is Alpha Omega, beginning & end the Great I AM! He is Lord of my life. I have decided that He will lead me in all things. The Holy Spirit was sent to be our comforter. I invite Him everyday to lead, guide me. I don't want to do anything that not inspired by God. If I try on my own where will that get me? But if I do what the Holy Spirit is telling me I am more than a conqueror! Who are you following?

God is Alpha Omega, beginning & end the Great I AM! He is the Lord of my life. I have decided that He will lead me in all things.

The Holy Spirit was sent 2 B our comforter. I invite Him everyday 2 lead, guide me. I don't want 2 do anything that not inspired by God.

If I try on my own where will that get me? But if I do what Holy Spirit is telling me I am more than a conqueror! Who are you following?

******

When you are in tuned with Holy Spirit, He is telling you things that others are hearing in the body of Christ. That is when you know that God is speaking. Are you seeking God and if so what has God been telling you?

R U tuned in to the Holy Spirit. Does it line up with what others are hearing in the body of Christ? That is when you know that God is speaking.

******

When problems come your way, you have a choice to make. Do I go this way and try to figure it out on my own, or do I stop and ask God what should I do? I am learning to rely on the Holy Spirit in all things. Sometimes it is hard and you want to react out of your flesh, but when I step back and pray and wait to hear from God, things happen. I can do all things through Christ who strengthens me.

R U at a crossroads? Learn to rely on the Holy Spirit. I have and it really works. It is hard sometimes, but it really works! God never fails!

******

Today I was reminded of all the things God has been telling me. He confirms thru prayer, scripture, prophets, His voice. How can you doubt when He is present everywhere? I know that He is faithful. He is going to lead us to the next level. Through him I have my being and I give God all the glory.

God confirms thru prayer scripture prophets & His voice How can U doubt He is everywhere? Thru him I have my being I give God all the glory

******

Being led by Holy Spirit daily requires work. You need to start your day with prayer/devotions. You need to press into the things of God. The effectual fervent prayer of a righteous man avails much. Prayer: You are talking to God. Being led by the Spirit: He is talking to you. Who are you talking to and who are you listening to?

Start your day prayer/devotions. U need 2 press into God. The effectual fervent prayer of a righteous man avails much.

When U pray U R talking to God. When U R being led by the Spirit He is talking 2 you. Who are you talking to and who are you listening to?

******

Today be led by the Holy Spirit. Let your day be filled with people who God leads you to. Listen to what the Holy Spirit has to say when you are with them. Try to be led by the spirit in all things. If you do that you can't go wrong. Who do you listen to?

Let your day B filled w people who God leads U 2. Hear what God has 4 them B led by the spirit. If U do that U can't go wrong

******

My prayer: God I want to know you more. Jesus I want to be more like you. Holy Spirit I want to follow you more. Lead guide and direct my day. Use me and stir up the gifts that you have given me. Bless me in all things

My prayer: God I want 2 know U more. Jesus I want 2 B like Holy Spirit I want 2 follow U more.

Lead guide and direct my day. Use me and stir up the gifts that you have given me. Bless me in all things

******

Where does God have you? Where do you fit in? If you don't know, ask God for direction for your life. Don't move without the Holy Spirit telling you to move. Use the talent that God has given you for His purpose.

Where does God have U? Where do U fit in? Ask God 4 direction Don't move without God telling U 2 move. Use what God has given U 4 His purpose

Tweets And Posts
(These Can Be Used For Both)

Walk in the Spirit and you will not fulfill the lusts of the flesh. You cannot stand still you either go backwards or forwards.

******

Karen Stone Janiczek

Section Five

FORGIVENESS

Sometime we have to agree to disagree! Life is too short to argue. Can't we just all get along? God forgives us no matter what and so should we forgive. If we don't forgive then are we saying we are higher or better than God?

Agee 2 disagree life is 2 short Can't we get along? Forgive God does!

******

Jealousy is a killer for relationships. Instantly rebuke those thoughts, No I will not entertain that! I love that person and want the best for them. We have the power to embrace or reject thoughts that Satan throws our way. I want to live in light not darkness. God is light and Satan is darkness.

Jealousy a killer for relationships. Rebuked that thought No I will not entertain that! I love that person and want the best for them.

We have the power 2 embrace or reject thoughts that Satan throws our way. I want2 live in light not darkness. God is light Satan is darkness.

******

A friend is someone who is there no matter what! In the good times and bad. Even when you are fighting with them they are there. Sometimes friends do not stick by you. Something happens and they fall away! But Jesus is our one true friend! He is there no matter what! You can rely on Him always! I am glad I have a friend in Jesus!

Friends can fall away but U can rely on Jesus He is always there. I am glad I have a friend in Jesus!

******

The only day you have is today. You never know what tomorrow will bring. Life is too short to be harboring bitterness un-forgiveness towards others. As Obi One said, "Let Go Luke!" Lay it all down at the cross of Jesus. Forgivingness=freedom. God cannot bless you with un-forgiveness in your heart.

Life is 2 short 2 B harboring bitterness un-forgiveness. As Obi One said, "Let Go Luke!" Lay it all down at the cross of Jesus.

Forgivingness=freedom. God cannot bless you with un-forgiveness in your heart.

******

Do not let hate and anger fester. Once you open that door it grows and grows and you have no peace. God cannot bless us when we have un-forgiveness in our hearts. Forgive now!

Do not let hate & anger fester. Once you open door it grows & U have no peace. God cannot bless with un-forgiveness in our hearts.

******

Can you or will you forgive? Big difference! Do we really want to forgive someone who has hurt us? The Bible says that we have to forgive others. Luke 6:37 "Do not judge, and you will not be judged. Do not condemn, and you will not be condemned. Forgive, and you will be forgiven." Sometimes you need to forgive yourself. Can you or will you forgive?

Can u or will U 4give? Big difference we do not want 2 4give those who hurt us. Luke 6:37 Sometimes U need 2 4give your self. Can U or will U 4give?

******

God is good all the time. No matter what! Forgiveness from God is just a breath away. God sent His only Son to die on the cross for our sins. Just invite Him into your life. It is that simple.

Forgiveness from God is just a breath away. God sent His Son 2 die on the cross 4 our sins. Just invite Him into your life It is that simple

******

Bitterness and anger leads to destruction. God cannot move in your life if you are harboring any un-forgiveness. It's the biggest thing that binds us. Forgiveness is from the Father. Peace comes.

Bitterness and anger leads to destruction. God cannot move The biggest thing that binds us. Forgiveness is from the Father. Peace comes.

******

Life is about choices. You choose who, what, where you go. You choose to be happy and to love or to be bitter and angry and to hate. What you choose defines who you are. You can make choices on your own or you can ask God. You choose!

Life is about choices What U choose defines who U R. U can make choices on your own or U can ask God. U choose!
******

Hatred is an emotion. Without forgiveness the roots of hatred and bitterness can run deep. Year after year of hatred digs in deeper and deeper. Hatred and un-forgiveness separates you from God. No good can come from hating. You can be kind to a complete stranger, yet hate a family member. Let's wake up and ask for forgiveness. God loves us all no matter what.

Without forgiveness the roots of hatred and bitterness can run deep & separates U from God. No good can come from hating. Forgive Now!

You can be kind to a complete stranger, yet hate a family member. Let's wake up and ask for forgiveness. God loves us all no matter what!
******

Your words are so important. You can curse or yell at someone, or you can be loving and supportive. You can also curse yourself with negative words or you can bless yourself with faith words. Are you lifting up or hurting someone? Life is too short! Work in love, not hate! Let your words guide who you are. Tell someone that you love them today! And remember Jesus loves you everyday!

Your words R so important. U can curse or bless. R U lifting up/hurting someone? Work in love, not hate! Let your words guide who you are.

Tell someone that you love them today! And remember Jesus loves you everyday!

******

Words can do many things. Words can hurt and offend. Words can heal and forgive. Words can be hateful or kind. What we have to remember is that they are just words. Sometimes you just have to look past what someone says and remember don't let other peoples words ruin your day or even your life.

Words can do many things Hurt offend hateful/heal kind forgive. Look past what some1 says Don't let peoples words ruin your day/life.

******

A person's spiritual maturity depends on your willingness to face, forgive and forget past offenses. Alot of times we judge ourselves by our intentions and judge everyone else by their actions. Just walk in love and don't react.

Spiritual maturity depend on willingness 2 forgive forget past offenses we judge ourselves by our intentions & judge others by their actions

******

It is unproductive & not easy to give it to God. We have been hurt so often that we build walls. People that hurt others grew up being hurt or watching others being hurt. But God will tear down those walls and show you His love.

It is unproductive & not easy to give it to God. We have been hurt so often that we build walls. Let God tumble those walls.

People that hurt others grew up being hurt or watching others being hurt. But God will tear down those walls and show you His love.

******

How are you feeling today? Are you grumpy and mad? Or happy and glad? It is your choice how you feel. It does not matter if someone did something to you. It is still your choice as to how you feel. Walk in love not in hate! Forgive and forget, I know that is what God does when we ask for forgiveness.

How R U feeling today? Your choice how U feel Turn other cheek. Walk in love not in hate! Forgive forget! God does when we ask 4 forgiveness.

Tweets And Posts
(These Can Be Used For Both)

Today is a day of remembrance. God is the healer of all hurts. Don't harbor any offences. Don't let un-forgiveness stop the blessings of God.

******

With God all things are possible. Don't let hate and unforgiveness stand in your way of receiving what God has for you.

******

Section Six

DAILY LIFE WITH GOD

Living each day without God is empty. Living each day with God is full. To know that God loves me each and every day is enough for me. But to know that Jesus died for my sins is joyous! To talk to God each day is a pleasure and to hear God's voice each day is a blessing. I am GBHF!

Day with out God:empty. Day with God:full. Jesus died 4 my sins:joyous. Hear God's voice:blessing. Gods love is enough 4 me.

******

Every day God blesses me. Every day He shows me that He loves me. Every day I see His goodness. Every day I Praise God. Everyday I read the Word. Every day I pray to God. What do you see every day? What do you do every day?

Every day God blesses shows me His love I see His goodness I Praise God read the Word pray. What do U do every day?

******

What does your day look like? Is it filled with drama and turmoil? Or order and peace? Don't be stressed out let God do the work. Give it over to God and then rest in His love. Who better to hand your problems over to. He knows all and wants the best for us!

Drama & turmoil from the devil! Order & peace from God! Hand your problems over 2 God and let Him give U peace!

******

Every day is filled with ups and downs. It's how you handle those ups and downs that count. I am choosing to turn to Jesus no matter what. On the mountain or in the valley, Jesus is my rock, my salvation. I will not waiver! I am greatly blessed and highly favored.

Life is ups & downs How U handle them that count. I am choosing 2 turn 2 Jesus. Jesus is my rock, my salvation. I will not waiver!

******

A lot of people look at Mondays as UGH!!! Monday! But I am looking at Monday as another week for God to bless us. Come on God, You are great and I am expecting great things from YOU.

Mondays UGH! I am looking at Monday as another week 4 God 2 bless us. U R great God I am expecting great things from YOU

******

Today things may look great then BAMMM! Something happens. Your whole world is upside down. How many realize that you are at a cross roads when that happens. You can look at the negative get all stressed out with worry. Or you can choose to look to God. Give it over to Him let Him give you peace. You will still be in the situation but you can go through it with God and His peace.

Life going great then BAM! Something happens! Your whole world is upside down. U R at a crossroads.

U can look at the negative stressed out with worry. Or U can look 2 God. Jesus gives you peace.

******

Every day you start new. New possibilities, new horizons. Yes you may have the old junk still nagging you but it is a new day and an new start. Start your day talking to God. Include Him. If you let Him lead and guide you and listen there is no better place to be. I know that God's ways are better ways. Just sayin'

Every day U start new, don't let the junk slow U down. Start your day with God He will lead U 2 new possiblities, new horizons.

******

It seems that each day flies by! Morning...then sleep! Day after day flying by faster and faster. What do you fill your days with? Wrong or right choices? Do you fill you day with me...me...me...or do you fill it with God?

Life is flying by! Days are flying by! What do you fill your days with? Wrong or right choices? Me...me...me...or God?

******

Today is a new day! Shake off yesterday go forward in the Lord! No weapon formed against me shall prosper! I am putting on the whole armor of God. Yes I fall short of the glory of God but the great thing is that God loves me no matter what and forgiveness is always there.

Today is a new day! Shake off yesterday go forward in the Lord! No weapon formed against me shall prosper!

I am putting on the whole armor of God I fall short of the glory of God but God loves me no matter what forgiveness is always there.

******

What does your day look like? Is it filled with drama and turmoil? Or order and peace? Don't be stressed out...let God do the work. Give it over to God and then rest in His love. Who better to hand your problems over to? He knows all and wants the best for us!

Is your day filled with stress? God has no-fault assurance. Cast your cares on Him for He cares for you. He will take care of your problems.

******

Everyday is a new adventure jump right in, but don't forget to bring God with you. Don't forget to let him lead you on your adventure. You can't go wrong by having God as your pilot.

Everyday new adventure. Don't forget 2 bring God with U. Let him lead on your adventure. U can't go wrong by having God as your pilot

******

Started my day with God, He showed up Big! Now as I go through the day it is fast pace and hectic, but there is an underlying peace that only God can give you. Oh...one more thing...I am greatly blessed and highly favored by God.

Start with God, Life is hectic but there can B an underlying peace that only God can give you.

******

This week has flown by! Everyday with God is a blessed day! Every day with Jesus is a great day! And everyday being led by the Holy Spirit is a smart day! What kind of day are you having?

Everyday with God blessed! Every day with Jesus great! And everyday being led by Holy Spirit is a smart day! What kind of day R U having?

******

Friday is here! The weekend approaches! Everyone knows their plans for Saturday, but do your plans for the weekend include God? Is church on your radar? Fellowshipping with God is important every day. Attending church is the icing on the cake.

Friday is here! The weekend approaches! Everyone knows their plans for Saturday, but do your plans for the weekend include God?

Is church on your radar? Fellowshipping with God is important every day. Attending church is the icing on the cake.

******

Going to church starts your week out right! Don't forget Him the rest of the week! You get fed at church; feed yourself with the Word of God daily. Fellowship with others is great, but fellowshipping with God is the best! So don't forget Jesus tomorrow, or the next...or the next day....

Going to church starts your week out right! Don't forget Him the rest of the week! U get fed at church; feed your self daily with the Word.

Fellowship with others is great, but fellowshipping with God is the best! So don't forget Jesus tomorrow, or the next or the next day

******

Busy busy busy! Today has been so busy. If our lives get too busy we could forget about God. I needed to stop & remember God several times during my day. Just remember to recognize God all day long.

Today has been so busy. If our lives get busy we could forget about God. Just remember to recognize God all day long.

Tweets And Posts
(These Can Be Used For Both)

Living in grace day by day. Living for God day by day. Living for Jesus day by day. Living with Holy Spirit day by day. What more is there?

******

Been so busy! All I can say is God is good...all the time...no matter what we are going through. God is good!

******

What a day...one of those days where it is hard to keep your testimony. But I will! By the grace of God!

******

In this hour God wants His people to stand confidently in their assignments, clothed in His power & grace.

What a beautiful day! God is on the throne and Jesus is alive! Sometimes you just have to thank Him for all He has done for you.

******

So much to do, so little time. But it is almost finished. Only have a few more things to do...Lord I call upon that restoration oil! Amen

Section Seven

LIFE

Life is short. We take for granted that we will be here another day. God has a plan for everyone and we need to find out what that plan is for our lives. If you don't know ask God and He will tell you. Start confessing the things of God. Use your faith every day!

Life is short. God has a plan for U we need 2 find out what it is Don't know ask God He will tell you.

Start confessing the things of God. Use your faith every day!

******

Life is coming at us so fast! It is always something! We need to slow down and find time for God. We find ourselves too busy for God, but God needs to be first in all things. Daily devotions, prayer, reading His Word and listening for Him to talk to us. Take the clutter out of your life and find time to be with God on a daily basis. Life will still be flying by but God can be the calm in the storm.

Take the clutter out of your life & find time 2 B with God daily Life will still be flying by but God can be the calm in the storm.

******

If you want to live well, make sure you understand all of this. If you know what's good for you, you'll learn this inside and out. God's paths get you where you want to go. Right-living people walk them easily; wrong-living people are always tripping and stumbling. Hosea 14:9 The Message

U want 2 live well make sure U know all of this If U know what's good for U, U'll learn this inside & out God's paths get U where U want 2 go

Right-living people walk them easily; wrong-living people are always tripping and stumbling. Hosea 14:9 The Message

******

Ever have a day where all is going great. God's blessing, then WHAM! Words are said you find yourself spiraling down a road you don't want to travel. Now a huge fight! Where is this coming from? The devil is crafty; he's out to destroy relationships! Take control recognize where it's coming from, come against it in the name of Jesus. God is peace not strife; he is love not anger Where do you walk?

Great day then WHAM! Words R said U find yourself spiraling down a road U don't want 2 travel. A huge fight! Where is this coming from?

The devil is crafty; he's out 2 destroy relationships! Take control recognize where it's coming from, come against it in the name of Jesus.

God is peace not strife; he is love not anger Where do you walk?

******

Things not going so well, but I will praise the Lord in all things. In all things! Even in the midst of a storm, I will Praise the Lord in all things!

Things not going so well I will praise the Lord in all things. Even in the midst of a storm, I will Praise the Lord in all things!

******

Have you ever had someone accuse you of something you are not? You ask others am I like that? They say no way! You know you're not like that! Usually the person doing the accusing they have the problem in their lives! Don't pull the splinter out of others when you have a beam in yours.

Someone accuse U of something U R not That person is usually looking in mirror. Don't pull splinter out of others when U have beam in yours!

******

Bullying has to stop! As children teens and adults. When someone is a bully it is because they want to feel superior to you. You just have to say, ENOUGH NO MORE! Don't let the words of others dictate who you are. God made you special.

Bullying has to stop! U have to say ENOUGH NO MORE! Don't let the words of others dictate who U R. God made U special!

******

Why do people young and old bully? It makes then feel important! It makes them feel good. They are not even aware of the hurt they are causing the other person. It is all about

82

them! Time to stand up to the bully in your life! Don't let anyone young or old bully you!!!

Why do people bully? 2 feel important & feel good. Time 2 stand up 2 the bully in your life! Don't let anyone young or old bully you!!!

******

Reality check. You can raise your children to know the Lord but when they become an adult they do what they want. Even though they are going down the wrong path, there is nothing you can do. You just have to love them & spend allot of time down on your knees.

Reality check. Raise your children 2 know God As adult they do what they want. Right/wrong path love them spend time down on your knees

******

God trusts us with our children and gives them to us raise. Then we let them go. They are not our children but God's. We have to trust God that He is watching over them even in tough times. Sometimes we have to demonstrate tough love. We love them so much we have to do things that at the time look mean but it is really love. Even God gives us correction and sometimes it really hurts but He loves us no matter what.

God gives us our kids to raise. Trust God is watching over them. They need 2 depend on God not U! It is called tough love! Even God uses it!

******

Raising children is easy, it is when they grow up that it becomes hard. But God is in control and I love my children beyond measure. I am proud of them every day!

God is in control and we need to let Him deal with our children when they R adults.

******

What is great about being a Christian? Knowing that Jesus is your personal Savior and that you have eternal life. Resting in God in all things. Trusting, believing, having peace through the storm. Talking to God, hearing His voice. Reading the Bible. Being led by the Holy Spirit. Fellowshipping with other believers. Knowing that God loves me no matter what I have done. Tell me why you love being a Christian. GBHF!

Great things about being a Christian: Rest, Trust, Faith; Peace; Prayer; Being led; Fellowship & knowing God's love. What is your list?

******

How many times in the day do you say, "Oh my God!" Let's think about this. Did it just come out? Ever watch a TV program when they are surprised they all say OMG! Is He really your God? Does Jesus live in your heart? Are you daily going to Him in prayer or reading your Bible? Let the words that come out of your mouth praise God. Not shock God!

Do U say, Oh my God? Too many people just blurb that out! Is He your God? Let your words that come out Praise God!

******

Are you a phony? Go around and say what people want to hear? Should you only say what is politically correct? Or should you just lie? Maybe saying nothing is the answer. Funny when a Christian has an opinion...they say you are judgmental. Or they say you are a hypocrite. They get offended and mad. Maybe people just don't want to hear the truth.

What comes out of your mouth? People R judging U by your words & actions.

******

Whoever said, "sticks and stones can break my bones, but words can never harm me" did not have a clue to the power of one's words. As we both know, words hold the power of life and death; we all need to put a watch on our lips and a guard on our hearts, and to be careful of whose Kingdom we represent by the things we say.

Words can hurt they have the power of life & death. Put a watch on your lips guard your heart. B careful whose Kingdom U represent.

******

Do you understand the gifts that God gave you? Are you growing in your gifting? Are you feeling confident in your gifting? Know that God gave you gifts and learn to work in them. Thank you God for blessing me with my gifting.

Understand your gifting & grow in it. Know that God gave U those gifts so learn to work in them 4 His glory.

******

When you're in the wilderness, turn around and see where you have been, then look where you're headed. Know that God is there in the wilderness. You may seem alone but He is there. Keep your eyes focused on Jesus. Let God work in the wilderness. But be willing to shed the old. Keep talking to Him and you will get through a better person.

Wilderness? Turn around see where U been but look forward see where you're headed. God is with U Focus on Jesus Shed the old embrace the new.

******

Where do you find yourself more? Things of the world, Alcohol, smoking, porn, hate? Or things of God, the Word, praying, love, forgiveness? Yes we all sin and come short of the Glory of God. But God is there to forgive and to love. What fruit are you producing?

Worldly things: Alcohol, smoking, porn hate. Godly things: prayer, love, bible, forgiveness We all have sin & come short of the Glory of God

******

God is there in the midst of the storm. God wants to be with you when you go through tough times. You need to reach out and tell Him. Give Him your burdens-hurts. Lay them at the cross and let God comfort you.

God is there in the midst of the storm. He is there in tough times. Give Him your burdens lay them at the cross

******

Proverbs 24: 17-18 "Don't rejoice when your enemies fall; don't be happy when they stumble. For the Lord will be displeased with you and will turn his anger away from them"

Prov 24:17-18 Don't rejoice when enemies fall don't B happy they stumble Lord will B displeased w U & will turn his anger away from them

******

When you are going through the valley, remember God is with you. When you are going through hard times, remember to praise Him no matter what. Even when you look around and only see despair. God never leaves you. Just reach out to Jesus. He is the answer every time. Praise Him in the good times and praise Him in the bad. Just Praise Him!!!

Praise God in the good & bad. God never leaves U Reach out 2 Him

******

When you are feeling down...prayer works. When things are troubling you...prayer works. When you are sick...prayer works. When you are at your wits end...prayer works. When you are happy...prayer works. Prayer works no matter what. But the question: are you praying at all? Try praying to God everyday no matter what and see how your life will change.

Feeling down: Prayer works Trouble times: Prayer works Sick: Prayer works End of your rope: Prayer works Happy: Prayer works

******

People who achieve high honors in their field are always praised. Like the Oscars, they thanking everyone. These people have achieved a high honor and should be praised. But what I thought, how much more does our Heavenly Father need and want to be praised and thanked. Just a thought!

People who achieve high honors R praised. How much more does our God need & want 2 B praised. Just a thought!

******

We all have a place in the body. And the talents that the Lord has given us we are not to bury it, but to take that talent and use it. What is your talent? And are you using it for God?

We all have a place in the body. What is yours?

Do not bury your talent. Use it 4 God. What is your talent? R U using it for Him?

******

When you look at things in the natural you may want to run and hide. But when you look at things through the eyes of Christ and you put all your cares on Him, then you have peace to go on through out your day. Cast all your cares upon Jesus and have peace.

Do U want 2 run & hide? Put your cares on Jesus. Have peace cast your cares upon Him.

******

Whenever I think about God I think about how much He loves us and that He is there everyday to guide and direct us. Some people think God is angry or He is just there but not available, He is a hand in a cloud, He is the pope. Some think He is a sugar daddy or not interested in our lives. And some don't even think He exists. Question: Who do you think God is and how does He work in your life?

Question: Who do you think God is and how does He work in your life?

******

Everyday we have to put on the armor of God. They fight off the fiery darts that come your way. Funny how people are usually the ones throwing those darts, even Christians. The Word says after you put on the armor to stand! Stand strong, no need to fight! I am standing and watching God fight my battles. Waiting for the victory through Christ. Are you standing or fighting?

Put on the whole armor of God. Then let God fight. Stand! Wait 4 the victory!

******

The fruit of righteousness will be peace; the effect of righteousness will be quietness and confidence forever. Is32:

17 When God is first in your life and you give Him total control, you have peace. So if you think you trust and totally surrender to God, but you are not at peace, or trying to figure it out on your own, then you need to search your heart. Have you totally given God everything?

The fruit of righteousness will be peace; the effect of righteousness will be quietness & confidence forever. Is32: 17 Have U totally given God everything?

******

You need to align yourself with the right people. Like minded in Christ. It is about right relationships in Christ. And I thank you Lord for those relationships that we have and that we will continue to have. God is not finished with us yet! If God is for you who can be against you? I am greatly blessed and highly favored of the Lord!

Align yourself with right people. Like minded in Christ. Right relationships. God is not finished with me yet.

******

I was just thinking on what God has brought me through. I learned: We all need to watch our thoughts because they become our words, we have to watch our words or they will become our actions, we have to watch our action or they will become our nature, and watch our nature or it will become our future.

We ned to watch our thoughts they become our words, watch words become actions, watch actions become nature, watch nature become future.

******

Someone said to me the other day. "I'm a Christian because I go to church" I said to them "Going to church doesn't make you a Christian just like standing in a garage doesn't make you a car" I know that's not very spiritual but it's the truth...

Going 2 church does not make U a Christian, just like standing in a garage does not make U a car. John 3:16
******

I have learned we have to encourage ourselves in the Lord when we make mistakes we can't quit but move forward. Because a person who never makes mistakes in their life looses the chance of learning something. We are not perfect. The key to everything is patience. God loves us all the time.

Patience is the key. Be encourage in the Lord. Don't quit but learn something.
******

God is calling those who seek Him to a higher level. Go deeper in Him. Those who diligently seek him will find His favor. Make sure you are in alignment with God so when the blessing flows you will be in His perfect alignment.

God is calling those to seek Him. Go deep in Him. Align with God. Perfect Alignment.
******

Ever clean out your house? Spring cleaning! You get rid of the old and clutter. Why hang onto stuff you don't need. Much like our lives we have stuff that we are clinging onto. Why? Start to clean out the stuff and with Gods help move on! It feels good to clean out the junk!

Clean out the junk in your life! Get the clutter gone! Don't hang onto the old! Move on with God it feels good!
******

Where are you today? Are you growing or are you withering? Maybe you are just existing? God will meet you at any stage of your life. He wants you to excell! He wants you to soar on wings of eagles! He wants you to walk in everything He has for you. I know that I want my storehouse in heaven to be empty. Won't need it in heaven.

Where R U today? Growing/withering? R U existing? God will meet U there. God wants U 2 excell soar on wings of eagles! Move with Him.

******

Tweets And Posts
(These Can Be Used For Both)

Wrong conduct is based on wrong believing. What kind of conduct do you have? What kind of belief do you have?
******

When someone's character is not clear to you look at their friends Don't judge but be a fruit inspector.
******

"His time" is time with God. Prayer, Praise and Bible time. How much "His Time" have you had lately.
******

Do you listen to one side of a story? One persons point of view? Then take sides! Repent! Get both sides. Don't judge

Section Eight

DESTINY
or
GOD'S PLAN
FOR YOUR LIFE

Expectations! What are you expecting God to do in your life? Rom 4:17 Call those things that be not as though they were. Speak your expectations! God wants to give you the desires of your heart. Ask...Seek...Knock! Then have faith. Now faith is the substance of things hoped for and the evidence of things not seen.

Expectations! What are you expecting God to do in your life? Rom 4:17 Call those things that be not as though they were.

Speak your expectations! God wants to give you the desires of your heart. Ask...Seek...Knock!

Then have faith. Now faith is the substance of things hoped for and the evidence of things not seen

******

Have you found your destiny? What did God create you to do? I don't think God wants us to just walk through life ups and downs, just existing. Do you know what He wants you to do? If you are clueless...ask God what is it you created me for? Ask, Seek, Knock!

Have you found your destiny? What did God create U 2 do? I don't think God wants us to just walk through just existing.

Do you know what He wants U 2 do? If U are clueless...ask God what is it U created me for? Ask, Seek, Knock!

******

Where is life taking you? Are you on your track or Gods? Is it your vision or Gods? Is God even in your path of life? Maybe you just exist? It is not too late to stop and regroup and ask God where do you want me to go? If you put God first and ask Him where, when, what? He will show you. Let God steer your ship not you!

Where is life taking U? U just exist? Your vision or Gods? Put God 1ˢᵗ ask Him where, when, what? He will show U. Let God steer the ship

******

What plans does God have for you? You were designed for a purpose in life. What is that purpose? Is it to be a mother and raise your children? Is it for you to be a CEO of a company? No matter what it is do your best in that calling. God will honor your faithfulness and He will give you more!

Gods plan 4 U? U have a purpose Is it 2 B a mother or CEO? Whatever it is do your best God will honor your faithfulness He will give U more

******

Time goes by so fast. As I look back I say, "Where did it go?" Funny time is important to us, but for God it is not. He was, He is and always will be. He wants us to find our destiny in Him, so we can accomplish what we were put on this earth to do. I know my destiny! Seek Him find out what you were made to do.

Time is important 2 us 4 God it is not He was, He is & always will be Find your destiny so U can accomplish it. Find out what U were made 2 do.

******

Being a Christian is who we are! Even though we are Christians we still live in this world and we still sin. But I strive everyday to have the mind of Christ. I am not perfect and never said I was but I am saved by grace and I know that God has a plan for my life.

Being a Christian is who we are! We still live in this world & still sin. I strive 2 have the mind of Christ.

I am not perfect never said I was but I am saved by grace and I know that God has a plan for my life.

******

Are you on the path that God wants you to be on? Are you leading God or following Him? Ask Him to lead and guide you daily. He cares that much for us that He will show us what path to take, we only have to ask! Oh yea then we have to listen!

What path R U? R U leading God or behind Him? U want Him 2 lead He cares & will show U the way. Ask listen!

******

God, I thank you for all you are doing in my life. Thank you for vision and destiny. Thank you Lord for supplying all of my needs. Thank you Lord for just being You. I thank you Lord in all things. Without You I am nothing. I find my being in you. I will Praise Your name forever!

God, I thank U for all U R doing. 4 vision Thank U 4 supplying all needs. Thank you Lord for just being You.

I thank you Lord in all things. Without You I am nothing. I find my being in you. I will Praise Your name forever!

******

God is moving in the body. We all have a part of that. Each a different part with a different mission that God has given us. We just need to stay focused on what God has for us.

We all have a part in the body. Each different with different mission that God has given us. We need 2 stay focused on God

******

I am reminded today that prayer is communication with God. Yes I know that. But sometimes we go to Him and say...me...me...me! We have to be pro-active in prayer. Not just going to God in our time of trouble, but go and praise Him, stand on the word, declare and decree! What do you want from God? Have you talked to Him about it? What has God told you?

Prayer is communication with God. It is not all about me! B pro-active in prayer. Not in our time of trouble, but praise Him.

Stand on the word, declare & decree! What do U want from God? Have U talked to Him about it? What has God told you?

******

Life is short what are you doing for God? He made you to do something for the kingdom of God. Find your destiny and purpose in Him and you will be fulfilled.

What R U doing for God? He made U 2 do something for the kingdom of God. Find your destiny & purpose in Him & U will be fulfilled.

******

Where is God leading you? Or are you leading Him? Or maybe He isn't even in the picture? Where is God in your life? 1st or last or not even on the radar? Seek ye first the kingdom of God and then all these things shall be added unto you.

Where is God in your life? 1st last not even on the radar? Seek ye first the kingdom of God & then all these things shall B added unto U

Where are you today? Are you where you want to be? Have you accomplished your goals? When you were young did you see yourself where you are now? Probably your answer was, "I have fallen short!" Fallen short in your eyes or the Lords? Ask God what He wants you to do with your life. Where does he want you to be...not where you want to be!

R U where U want to B? Or have U fallen short? God will meet U where Rr at!

******

Tweets And Posts
(These Can Be Used For Both)

Who am I? I am no mistake! I have a purpose! No life is perfect! God loves me! And God has so much in store for me to come!!!!

******

Sometimes we question things in life but I have to remember why do I worry? I know God has a plan for everything!

******

God, I thank you for all you are doing in our lives, for our vision and destiny, for supplying all of our needs and for just being you.

******

I thank you Lord in all things. Without You I am nothing. I find my being in you. I will Praise Your name forever!

******

Section Eight

STUCK IN THE SAME THING

How long are you going to be stuck in your muck? How long are you going to hang onto your bitterness? How long defines who you are. How long causes strife and chaos. Let go of the how long...do it NOW! Decide today that you have had enough and step out of your how long! Jesus is there to meet you wherever you are. You have to take the first step!

How long R U going 2 B stuck in your muck? R U going B bitter? How long defines who U R Let go NOW! Jesus is there U take the first step!

******

Ever do renovations in your house? Tearing down a wall is hard work, tearing down walls in our lives is also hard work. Wall down now you have a mess to clean up, is there a mess in your life? You need to clean it up to move on. It maybe painful but God will restore. Renovations in your life lead to restoration. Upside, beautiful room...upside you can have beauty and victory in your life! Both take work!

Ever do renovations in your house? Tearing down a wall is hard work, tearing down walls in our lives is also hard work.

Renovations is messy is there a mess in your life? Clean it up 2 move on. It maybe painful but God will restore.

Renovations in your life lead 2 restorations. Upside, beautiful room...upside you can have beauty & victory in your life! Both take work!

******

What makes today different from yesterday? We do the same things everyday. Are you in the same mess you were in last year? Talk to God. Tell Him your hurts/troubles. He is your comforter. God is new every morning. YOU are the one who has to change, not God. YOU have to stop the sin & with God's help you will get through it. YOU are in the situation because of YOU not God but He will help you through.

What makes today different from yesterday? We do the same things everyday. Are you in the same mess you were in last year? Talk to God.

Tell Him your hurts/troubles. He is your comforter. God is new every morning. U R the 1 who has 2 change, not God.

YOU have to stop the sin & with God's help U will get through it. YOU R in the situation because of YOU not God but He will help U through.

******

Life is a bunch of choices. Should I go this way? No this looks better! Wait maybe my friends are right! STOP! Before you make any decisions talk to God. Ask Him what you should do. He will guide direct you. If you are hearing one thing and someone who you think is wiser than you says no go this way. STOP once again listen to the only voice that counts. GOD'S

Life is a bunch of choices. Should I go this way no this looks better! Maybe my friends R right! STOP! Before U make decisions talk 2 God

Ask Him what U should do. He will guide direct you STOP listening to everyone else listen 2 voice that counts. GOD'S

******

When you fall stand back up dust yourself off figure out why you fell. Turn around look behind you to see what made you fall, but then turn around look forward and determine that you won't fall again. Go forward with God. Give Him your worries; problems lay them at the cross. Let God be your leader. Follow the voice of the Holy Spirit. He will help you not fall, but you have to determine not to fall too.

When U fall stand back up figure out why U fell. Turn around look behind U 2 see what made U fall, look 4ward B determine U won't fall again

Go forward with God. Give Him your worries; lay them at the cross. Let God be your leader.

Follow the voice of the Holy Spirit. He will help you not fall, but you have to determine not to fall too.

******

Why do some people always lie? No matter what, their first response is, "Not me, I didn't do that." Even when the evidence points to them. Fess up to what you have done. It builds character and people will trust you. But once again you are on that merry go round. You have to jump off and say, NO MORE!

Why do people lie? Fess up It builds character & people will trust U.

******

Start tearing down your strongholds. Start replacing them with blessings. Are you on a merry go round year after year? That is a strong hold. Start tearing down generational curses or any curses that you may have brought on yourself. The enemy wants you to fail but God wants you to win. Start saying I am greatly blessed highly favored! Without faith it is impossible to please God.

Start tearing down your stronghold. Replace them with blessings. On a merry go round year after year? Tear down generational curses.

The enemy wants U 2 fail God wants U 2 win. Start saying I am greatly blessed highly favored! Without faith it is impossible 2 please God

******

Do you ever feel like you are on a merry go round? Different situations same results? Time to get off that merry go round? Simple, just give it over to Jesus. Leave it at the cross. Then when you get back on, turn to God and see what He will do.

Different situations same results? Time 2 stop! Give it 2 Jesus. Leave it at the cross. Turn 2 God see what He will do.

******

Isn't it time for Christians to be the head and not the tail? God is a rewarded of those who diligently seek Him. Start seeking God and stop doing it on your own. Get off your Merry Go Round and trust God. Be all in for God!

Isn't it time 4 Christians 2 B the head not the tail God rewards those who diligently seek Him. Start seeking God stop doing it on your own.

******

Spring has arrived! Time to clean and air out the house! Spring cleaning! Why don't you take time to clean out your life? Clean out the junk that is holding you back! You know the stuff that occurs over again and you say, I am not going to do that again!   "NO MORE!" With God's help you can do anything!

Spring cleaning! Time 2 clean & air out the house! Take time 2 clean out your junk NO MORE! With God's help you can do anything!

******

The best laid plans are meant to be interupted! And the kicker is to respond to the chaos in love! Just roll with it. It is all good. When you come up against your flesh tell it to die and follow the Holy Spirit in all things. You can't go wrong! God knows better than us. I want to pass the tests not keep taking the same test over and over again!

When we fail, we need to respond in love! When you come up against your flesh tell it to die and follow the leading of the Holy Spirit.

******

How long are you going to sit in your mire of self pity? Someone hurt you or stab you in the back? You choose how long you stay there. I have chosen to step out of it and forgive and forget! It happened yesterday and today I am over it! That is fast! Recognize it and move on!

Been hurt by someone. Choose to let it go. Forgive and forget! I was hurt yesterday and today I am over it! Recognize it and move on!

******

Where are you? Are you in the same place you were last year? Are you moving forward in God and birthing new things? Are you going backwards and letting the devil rob you of what God has for you? The Bible says we either go backwards or forwards, we cannot stand still. Where are you?

In the same place U were last year? R U moving forward doing new things? R U going backwards letting the devil rob U of what God has 4 U?

******

The Bible says you are either going forward or backward. You can't stand still. So are you truly going forward? Do you find yourself in the same situation over and over again? If so I would have to say you are not going forward. But if you are walking with God He will help you walk forward. All you have to do is trust and lean on Him. Let this year be a year of going forward, not backwards.

R U going forward or backward? R U in the same situation U always in? Stop & figure out why? Trust & lean on Him.

******

I know that no matter what I do God loves me and always will, but when I know it and intentionally do wrong. I don't like myself and I must live wth it. People say why did GOD punish me???? GOD doesn't punish you, people punish you or you punish yourself.

When U do wrong God still loves U. God does not punish us when we do wrong. We punish ourselves. God forgives…

******

Karen Stone Janiczek

Section Nine

THE DEVIL DEFEATED

The devil is crafty! He came to kill, steal and destroy! But my God is bigger! Devil get under my feet where you belong! I am greatly blessed highly favored, full of the anointing, anything I put my hand to will prosper and I walk in the fullness of God's plan for my life! Thank you God!

The devil came 2 kill steal & destroy! But my God is bigger! Devil get under my feet where you belong!

******

When the devil hits you he hits hard. But I am strong in God, no weapon formed against me shall prosper! I am the righteousness of God in Christ Jesus. I am mighty in God. Take that Satan! You are not going to get me riled up! I have the peace of God in all things.

The devil hits hard. I am strong no weapon formed against me shall prosper! I am the righteousness of God in Christ Jesus Take that Satan!

******

Luke 6:43-45 "A good tree doesn't produce bad fruit; on the other hand, a bad tree doesn't produce good fruit. Each tree is known by its own fruit. Figs aren't gathered from thorn bushes, or grapes picked from a bramble bush. A good man produces good, out of the good storeroom of his heart. An worldly man produces evil out of the evil storeroom, for his mouth speaks from the overflow of the heart."

******

Do you ever feel like giving up? There is no way out! You look around and you are drowning in life! No matter what you do you can't seem to find peace! Turn completely to Jesus. Not Jesus when I need Him, but totally all. Don't play church, but live the Living Word daily. That may require changes in your life, but you will not have total peace until you surrender to Him totally!

Ever feel like giving up? No way out! U R drowning in life! No matter what you do you can't seem to find peace! Turn completely to Jesus.

Don't play church, but live the Living Word daily. Not just Jesus when I need Him, but totally all in to Him.

******

Lord I am trying not to react but to be proactive. I want to be on the offensive not the defense. Meaning that I want to be aggressively pursuing the Lord. I do not want to only go to God when I am in trouble or out of my need. All in all the time. That way when things are thrown in my way it will not rattle me or shake me. My foundation is in God and no matter what I will not waiver!

Don't react but 2 B proactive. B on the offensive not the defense. Meaning that I want to be aggressively pursuing the Lord.

When things R thrown in my way it will not rattle shake me. My foundation is in God & no matter what I will not waiver!

******

It feels like fall this morning! But later it will feel like summer! Things are not always what they seem. The devil is crafty and things that may appear to be from God are not always from God. You need to be in tune with the Holy Spirit to know when God is moving in your life. Start talking to God and see where He leads you.

The devil is crafty things may appear 2 B from God R not always from God Tune 2 Holy Spirit 2 know when to move see where He will lead U

******

What has the devil stole from you? Finances relationships health? Step up tell the devil to stop! He is under our feet. All he can do is tempt you with suggestion. Tell him that you can no longer torment me. I am a child of the King. Break the strongholds; start confessing the blessings of God. I am healed, relationships restored, my bank account is full. Every day and don't stop till you see results.

Devil stole from U? Tell him stop He is under our feet Im child of the King. Break strongholds confess blessings don't stop till U C results

******

Sometimes life is hard. The enemy is crafty but I have reminded him that he is under my feet. I am more than a conqueror. I am the head, not the tail. So get thee behind me

Satan. Jesus is Lord, I am victorious in all things! I am greatly blessed, highly favored, full of the anointing, anything I put my hand to will prosper! Take that Satan!

Life hard enemy crafty Devil under my feet. I am more than a conqueror. I am the head, not the tail. So get thee behind me Satan.

Jesus is Lord, I am victorious in all things! I am greatly blessed, highly favored Take that Satan!

******

It does not take much to get riled up and frustrated! But recognize the attack from the enemy much sooner. God's peace is so calming. No weapon formed against me shall prosper. Devil give back what you have stolen from me in Jesus name! Thank you Lord for blessing me.

It does not take much to get riled up & frustrated! Recognize the attack from the enemy. God's peace is so calming.

No weapon formed against me shall prosper.

Devil give back what you have stolen from me in Jesus name! Thank you Lord for blessing me.

******

Funny how the devil try's to run havoc in your life. Well really it's not funny. Recognize the attack from the enemy much faster. Don't let it get you riled up come against the attack know that God is victorious! Remember the devil is under our feet. Remind him of that! We are joint heirs with Jesus! No weapon form against us shall prosper!

Devil try's 2 run havoc in your life. Recognize the attack Don't get riled up know that God is victorious joint heirs with Jesus!

******

What the enemy meant for bad God can turn it around and use it for good. All things work for good for those who Love the Lord. Stand on His word we are on the winning side.

What the enemy meant 4 bad God can turn it around & use it 4 good All things work 4 good 4 those who Love the Lord. Were on the winning side

******

Ever find yourself going through life and WHAM! This past week has been my WHAM week. I was hit HARD! I cried, felt sorry for myself, and a myriad of emotions! I finally realized the devil was attacking me. So instead of having a pity party, I started to say, the joy of the Lord is my strength, devil you are under my feet. No weapon formed against me shall prosper. I am joint heirs with Jesus. And I am feeling better!

My WHAM week Hit HARD! Say, the joy of the Lord is my strength, devil under my feet Joint heirs w Jesus. U will start feeling better

The devil tries to come at U from all angles. I am the righteousness of Christ Jesus. I know that I am the head not the tail I am GBHF!

******

Evil vs Good. Who wins? I know that my God is the God of the universe He will triumph over everything. Sometimes situations in life become a spiritual battle. Not person vs person, family member vs family member, situation vs situation but it runs deeper. Sometimes it's evil vs good. Devil vs God. My situation God will be victorious. That evil will bow to good. That my God is God!

******

Many times in our lives we do things we regret or want to forget. The devil has a way of reminding us of them daily. When we ask God's forgiveness He forgives us and He forgets the deed. We are the ones punishing ourselves for things of the past. Stop letting the devil torment you of your past. God forgives us, move on to bigger and better things in Christ.

Do U regret things? God forgives & forgets. We should do the same. Stop letting the devil torment U over past events. Move on

******

Boy, the enemy is on full attack! He knows that something is stirring in the heavenlys. Get thee behind me Satan and watch what my God is going to do!

The enemy is on full attack! He knows that something is stirring in the heavenlys. Get thee behind me Satan watch what God is going 2 do!

******

The weapons of our warfare are not carnal but they are mighty to the pulling down of strongholds. And no weapon formed against me shall prosper. Devil look out! You have no place in my family!

The weapons of our warfare R not carnal but they R mighty to the pulling down of strongholds. Devil look out! You have no place in my family!

******

Declaration: The Lord will deliver me from every evil work and preserve me for His heavenly kingdom. To Him be glory forever and ever. Amen. Ps 121:7-8 I am standing on that promise.

Declaration: The Lord will deliver me from every evil work & preserve me 4 His heavenly kingdom. To Him B glory forever and ever Ps 121:7-8

******

When a diaster hits, people often say, "why does God let this happen?" We live in a world where satan has dominion. Isaiah 14:12-15. But Jesus has defeated the devil and he is under our feet, and as Christians we can take authority over him. But now we can pray for the people.

When a diaster hits, people often say, "why does God let this happen?" We live in a world where satan has dominion. See Isaiah 14:12-15.

******

God is good all the time no matter when, where or why. Yea though I walk through the valley I will fear no evil. He is there in the valley just recognize your enemy come against him in Jesus name. Keep your eyes on Jesus as you walk through the storm. Remember we are more than conquerors joint heirs with Jesus. The same spirit that raised Christ from the dead dwells in me. What more do you need?

Yea tho I walk thru the valley I will fear no evil. He is there in the valley. Same spirit that raised Christ from the dead dwells in me.

******

Tweets And Posts
(These Can Be Used For Both)

Satan you will not interrupt what God has for us. We will overcome!

******

The weapons of our warfare are not carnal but to the pulling down of strongholds. Take control of your life and pull those strong holds down.

******

Another day...another victory! Devil you loose...God wins, so I win! You can't touch me! My God is bigger than anything!

******

When you battle the evil one you grow weary but Jesus is stronger than him. Let God take control and fight the battle for you!

******

The weapons of our warfare are not carnal but they are mighty to the pulling down of strongholds. What stronghold are you pulling down?

******

We need to wake up and say NO MORE! Satan is having a field day in our churches. NO MORE!!!

******

Look out devil I am on the run! There is no stopping me now!

******

It is just like the devil to throw havoc your way. Do not let the enemy get you down. No matter what we are GBHF!

******

Section Ten

JOY OF THE LORD

The Joy of the Lord is my strength! When things get you down, just say that a few times until you feel Gods joy. You may not feel like saying it but do it anyway! The Joy of the Lord is my strength!

The Joy of the Lord is my strength! R U down say that a few times until U feel Gods joy. U may not feel like saying it but do it anyway!

******

Ever feel just plain yucky! Is that a word? Anyway, when you are feeling like that, tell the devil to get under your feet where he belongs. And start to say, "The Joy of the Lord is my strength!" Until your yuckyness is gone. Is that a word? Anyway be blessed!

Ever feel just plain yucky! Feel like that, start to say, The Joy of the Lord is my strength! Until your yuckyness is gone. Is that a word?

******

God is good and faithful all the time. I am rejoicing today for His goodness! When one prays expect answers! God is in the answering prayer business. Try it and see!

God is good & faithful Rejoicing today 4 His goodness! When U pray expect answers! God is in the answering prayer business. Try it & see!

******

I am full of the joy of the Lord! I have a great bubbling in my spirit of good things to come. The Joy of the Lord is my strength! I know that My God shall supply all of my needs in Christ Jesus. God loves me no matter what! It is good Yes it is good!

I am full of joy! The Joy of the Lord is my strength! I know that My God shall supply all of my needs in Christ Jesus. It is good yes it is good!

******

Today is the day that the Lord has made, I will rejoice and be glad in Him. Business is blessed. Going to the next level! That is my confession and I am sticking with it!

Today is the day that the Lord has made, I will rejoice & B glad in Him. Going 2 the next level! That is my confession I am sticking with it!

******

I am blessed and highly favored. No weapon formed against me shall prosper. I am the head and not the tale. I can do all things through Christ, which strengthens me. And the Joy of the Lord is my strength!

Blessed highly favored. I can do all things through Christ, which strengthens me. And the Joy of the Lord is my strength!

Vacation over back to work. Vacations are great, they give you a time to relax and have fun. God never takes a vacation! He is there all the time for us. He is there to help us everyday. He wants to see us succeed and He wants to see us happy. Remember the Joy of the Lord is our strength! Where does your strength come from?

Vacations are great, they give you time 2 relax have fun. God never takes a vacation! He is there all the time 4 us. He is there 2 help

He wants 2 see us succeed & B happy. Remember the Joy of the Lord is our strength! Where does your strength come from?

******

What does God have in store for you? I am expecting great things! No matter where you are or what you are going through God is still on the throne. Feeling down, the Joy of the Lord is your strength. Need a breakthrough, Call those things that be not as tho they were. God loves you and wants the best for you. Just call it!

What does God have for you? I am expecting great things! No matter where you are God is still on the throne.

Feeling down, the Joy of the Lord is your strength.

Need a breakthrough? Call those things that be not as tho they were. God loves you and wants the best for you. Just call it!

******

This is the day that the Lord has made, I will rejoice and be glad in it! The Joy of the Lord is my strength! In everything give Praise! I'm just saying and declaring!

This day the Lord made I will rejoice & B glad in it The Joy of the Lord is my strength In everything give Praise Just saying & declaring!

******

Ever feel down? Like the worlds crashing in around you? That there is no hope? Where do I turn? I remember that the Joy of the Lord is my strength. I go to the cross and lay down my burdens there. Let Jesus take all your worries away. Let Jesus into your life and let Him be the Lord of your life.

Feel down? Worlds crashing in around U? No hope? Where do I turn? Go 2 the cross lay down burdens there. Jesus takes your worries away.

******

Things going bad? Don't feel like Praising God? Not happy? It says in the Bible, in everything give thanks. So I praise and worship you Lord. I am giving thanks in all things! Even this! Still GBHF, full of the anointing and anything I put my hand to will prosper!

Things going bad? Don't feel like Praising God? Not happy? It says in the Bible, in everything give thanks. I praise and worship you Lord.

When you are going through a trial. Keep your eyes on Jesus. Even when you feel like you are sinking and there is no hope. Keep your eyes on Jesus. Go to Him and just tell Him. "Help I need you. This seems impossible." God is a God of possible. Faith will see you through and remember the joy of the Lord is your strength!

Going through a trial. Keep your eyes on Jesus. U feel like U R sinking there is no hope. Keep your eyes on Jesus. Tell Him. Help I need U.

God is a God of possible. Faith will see you through and remember the joy of the Lord is your strength!

Tweets And Posts
(These Can Be Used For Both)

This is the day that the Lord has made, I will rejoice and be glad in it. Beautiful day The Joy of the Lord is my strength!

******

This is the day that the Lord has made I will rejoice and be glad in it!

******

When U R feeling frustrated just give it to God. Leave it at the cross let God deal with it. Remember the Joy of the Lord is your strength.

******

Karen Stone Janiczek

Section Eleven

OPEN DOORS

When the Lord tells you to do something and you act on it...look out! Things go fast! Let this week be a whirlwind of blessings. Thank You Lord! Walking through open doors!

When the Lord tells U 2 do something act on it. Let this week B a whirlwind of blessings. Thank You Lord! Walking through open doors!

******

Doors are opening walk through. The devil is mad! Doing the work of God is not always easy. When you start to walk into your destiny in God the enemy does not like it. Turmoil starts! He tries to get you to stumble. But I will not be swayed! I am more than a conqueror! I will follow Jesus no matter what!

Doors opening walk through. Doing the work of God is not always easy. I will not be swayed no matter what I will follow Jesus!

When U start 2 walk in 2 your destiny the enemy does not like it. Turmoil starts! He tries to get U 2 stumble. I am more than a conqueror!

******

Work can be exhausting. Things are fast paced. When God tells you to do something and then He opens the doors for you, you know that it is God. Just move forward following the Holy Spirit!

Work exhausting. Things R fast paced. God tells U 2 do He opens doors U know that it is God. Just move forward following the Holy Spirit

******

Thank you God for your blessings. Thank you for your goodness, thank you for your guidance. We are walking where you want us to walk. Open doors Lord and we will walk through! I love and Praise Your Name!

Thank U God 4 blessings goodness guidance. Walking where U want us 2 walk. Open doors Lord we will walk through! I love and Praise Your Name!

******

Had such a great day! God is blessing us. Thank you Lord for open doors and opportunities for us to walk through. You lead and we will follow. Walk in the Spirit and you will not fulfill the lusts of the flesh.

Thank U Lord 4open doors opportunities 2 walk through. You lead we follow. Walk in the Spirit & U will not fulfill the lusts of the flesh.

******

Tweets And Posts
(These Can Be Used For Both)

What is God telling you? Are you listening?

******

What a great day! Doors opening and walking through! I am GBHF!

******

Open Doors...Open Doors...Open Doors...Walking through...Walking through...Walking through...Thank U Lord...Thank U Lord...Thank U Lord!

******

Thank you God for your blessings, goodness and guidance. We are walking where you want us to walk. Open doors and we will walk through!

******

God is so good. Just listen to the voice of God to lead you through out your day. Again be led by the Holy Spirit.

******

Karen Stone Janiczek

Section Twelve

HOLIDAYS

3 John 1:2 Beloved I wish above all things that you prosper be in health, even as your soul prospers. Notice it says you may prosper and be in health even as your soul prospers. Start digging into the Word of God and start praying. Get the ball rolling and prosper!

3 John 1:2 Beloved I wish above all things that U prosper B in health, even as your soul prospers. Start digging into the Word and praying.

******

What is the New Year saying to you? Diet, exercise, new job, children, marriage? Don't forget to put God on that list. God first and you can't loose. Acts 17:28 For in Him we live and move and have our being.

New Year's list? Is God on that list? Acts 17:28 For N Him we live & move & have our being.

******

As you reflect back on the year think of the good times. Take the bad times and learn from them. Go forward, it is a year of right alignment and getting into position for God to bless you. Start confessing the impossible and see what God will do for you in this New Year. Don't doubt Now faith is the substance of things hoped for and the evidence of things not seen.

Reflect back but move forward this year Bad times learn from them. Right alignment get into position. Start confessing don't doubt have faith

******

Happy New Year everyone. Expect a great year! What does God want for you this year? Have faith that He will be faithful to complete it in you. Remember without faith it is impossible to please God. Let God guide your life instead of you. Be blessed!

Happy New Year! Expect a great year! What does God want 4 U this year? Use your faith & let God guide U

******

God is so good. New Year will be a year of blessings. We are calling those things to be not as though they were! We are greatly blessed and highly favored by God. Why don't you do the same and see what God will do!

New Year new blessings. Ask God then exercise your faith

******

A new year is approaching. Everyone makes New Years resolutions they usually don't keep. Why not this year surrender your heart to Jesus. It is simple all you have to do is invite Him to be Lord of your life. No change in your life is needed. He takes us just as we are. Don't let another year pass. Life is too hard without God.

Make 1 New Year's resolution that will keep. Surrender to Jesus and ask Him into your hearts.

******

Reflect back...look forward. There is no rear view mirror with God. He has forgiven and He has forgotten your sin. So reflect back...but look forward!

Reflect back look forward There is no rear view mirror w God. He has forgiven & He has forgotten your sin. So reflect back but look forward

******

God is calling those who seek Him to a higher level. This year will be one of going deeper in Him. Those who diligently seek him will find His favor. Make sure you are in alignment with God so when the blessing flows you will be in His perfect alignment.

New Year let Him take U 2 a higher level. Go deeper in Him. Right alignment Diligently seek Him.

******

Happy New Year! Let this be a year of getting in alignment to the blessings of God. I am expecting great things from God this new year! Be blessed!

Happy New Year! Let this B a year of getting in alignment 2 the blessings of God. Expect great things from God this new year! Be blessed!

******

Take this week to reflect what God has done in your life. Thank Him for all He has done. Then ask God what He has planned for your life. Then thank Him for all that He is going to do.

Reflect on what God has done. Thank Him. Ask Him what's next? Thank Him 4 what He is going 2 do.

******

Looking for a goal for 20 ? Start quoting this scripture 3 John 1:2 Beloved, I wish above all things that thou mayest prosper and be in health, even as thy soul prosper. Notice it says you may prosper and be in health, EVEN as your soul prospers. Start digging into the Word of God and start praying and your soul will prosper. And that starts the ball rolling for the rest.

Goals? 3 John 1:2 Beloved I wish above all things that U prosper & B in health even as your soul prospers.

******

I love Christmas time; it's the best time of the year! Wait who sang that? Johnny Mathis? Anyway, God is so good! Thank you God for sending your son Jesus for us!

Christmas time best time of year! Thank U God 4 sending your son Jesus for us!

******

Christmas time is a time of love. A time for family. A time for coming together and forgiving those who have hurt you. It reminds me of the story of Joseph in the Bible, how his brothers did terrible things to him, yet he forgave them. Life is too short for fighting and harboring un-forgiveness. Forgive, move on!

Christmas is a time 4 love & family. Coming together & Forgiveness Don't fight this holiday season. Jesus is the reason 4 the season!

******

Have you heard that saying Merry Christmas is taboo! Things are getting way out of hand in America! Kids can't wear red or green clothing to school this time of year! Can't have any signs of Christmas! Have to say Happy Holidays! What happened to freedom of speech, and religious freedom? All I can say is...Merry Christmas...Merry Christmas...Merry Christmas...Jesus is Born!!!!!!!!!!!!!!

Merry Christmas is taboo! Can't have Jesus in schools. Must say Happy Holidays! NOT! Merry Christmas Merry Christmas Merry Christmas

******

Even though it is cold outside, don't let the cold in your heart rule you. Christmas is a time of love and laughter. A time for family! If you have ought against someone tis the season to forgive. Jesus came into this world to pay the price for our sins. If God can forgive us, we should be able to do the same! Don't let hate spoil Christmas for you.

Cold outside don't let the cold in your heart rule U Have ought forgive especially family. This is a time 4 family. Jesus came 4 forgiveness

******

Is God real? Yes, you only need faith to believe. He will meet you where you are at. God loves you no matter what. Christmas is the season to celebrate the birth of Jesus Christ. I choose to say...Merry Christmas...not happy holidays.

Is God real? U only need faith 2 believe. God loves U Celebrate the birth of Christ this season.

******

Turkey day has passed and the day is gone, now onto Christmas! In all the hustle and bustle don't forget that

Christmas is all about the birth of Jesus. Santa and his elves are nice, but Jesus is why we celebrate this season.

Santa & his elves are nice, but Jesus is why we celebrate this season!

When is God good? All the time. When do you pray to Him? All the time. When do you talk to God? All the time. If you are having problems in your life then maybe you are not praying or talking to Him enough. During this busy season take time to pray and talk to God. His son is the reason for this celebrating season. Stop and take time to make room for Him.

Stop & make time and room 4 Jesus during this busy season of Christmas. He is good all the time. Pray and talk to God all the time.

******

Today I heard that 68% of family members will fight at Thanksgiving! That number is terrible. They said most of that was contributed to too much alcohol. Be responsible this holiday season because fighting with people you love can lead to bitterness and years of separation. I say this in love and not in judgment.

68% of families will fight this Thanksgiving. Most due 2 alcohol Be responsible fights can lead 2 years of fighting. Say I love U & don't judge.

******

Turkey Day weekend! Lot's of shopping and parties. Show love when standing in lines. Watch your mouth and what you say to others. God is love remember that!

Turkey Day weekend! Shopping & parties. Show love when standing in lines. Watch your mouth what U say 2 others. God is love remember that!

******

Today is Veterans Day. Thank you to all who have served in our military. And thank you to all the spouses as well. Those that I know personally, *(List those who you know who have served here)* thanks for defending our country. I am proud to say that I know you.

Veterans Day thank U 2 all who have served in our military! And 2 the spouses as well. I am proud 2 say I know U

******

Thank you to all of our veterans who served our country. You are the reason that we are free today. God Bless all of you. Our prayers are with you and your families today. Be blessed.

Thank U Vets U R the reason we R free today. God bless you & your families

******

Today is the National Day of Prayer for our Nation. All Christians need to pray for our president (even if you don't like him) and to pray for our leaders. So if nothing else take time out of your busy schedule and pray for our country. God is in control of everything.

National Day of Prayer so pray 4 our President & leaders. Pray 4 our country. God is in control.

******

Good Friday The day we remember that Jesus was crucified. God's only Son born of a virgin lived 33 sinless years, did many miracles, was brought through the streets and up the hill with his cross after being whipped. This was all part of God's plan. Jesus was the ulitmate and last sacrifice to pay for our sins. His blood was shed for our sins. Ask Jesus into your heart today.

Good Friday the day Jesus was crucified. Jesus was the ulitmate & last sacrifice 2 pay 4 our sins, His blood was shed 4 our sins.

******

Today is a celebration! Jesus died on the cross for our sins and on the third day he rose again. He defeated death and the grave. He got the keys from Satan and set the captives free. He died for your sins. Just ask Jesus into your heart today. He is there for you. Happy Easter, He has risen!

Celebrate Jesus died on the cross & rose on the 3ʳᵈ day He defeated death He died 4 our sins. Happy Easter He is risen!

******

Easter is this week and the next few days people will be thinking about church. Let people know what Jesus did for them. That they are set free!

Easter week & the next few days people will B thinking about church. Let people know what Jesus did for them. That they are set free

******

God is love! No matter what the situation is God is love! Through hate, despair, peace or calm...God is love! This week God sent His only Son to die for us! Jesus paid the price for our sins, so we could have life eternal with God. Now that is love!

Through hate, despair peace or calm God is love. God loved us He sent His Son 2 die on the cross 4 our sins so we can eternal life.

******

Halloween, the day we celebrate evil. We dress up, have parties, give candy, decorate houses all to give due to the devil. Don't hear anyone complaining about that, but when we celebrate the birth of Christ we are persecuted. Can't say Merry Christmas, no nativity scenes, don't mention Jesus in school! Doesn't America have it backwards? Today when we give out candy, tell the children "Jesus Loves You."

America has it backwards We celebrate Halloween but can't mention Christ! When U give out candy today say "Jesus loves U"

******

Today is Yom Kippur, the day of atonement of sins for Jews. Essentially it was for the forgiveness of sins for the next year. But Jesus came one time to forgive us of sin. He does not have to go to the cross every year. No, just one time. How much God loved us to send His Son for us. How much do you love God? Enough to ask Jesus into your heart and be Lord of your life?

Yom Kippur Day of Atonement, Old Testament. New Testament, Jesus atone 4 our sins. Live in grace not the law!

******

Tweets And Posts
(These Can Be Used For Both)

Merry Christmas! Have a blessed day and remember that Jesus is the reason for this day. Have fun!

******

New Year! Diet, exercise, new job, children, marriage? Don't forget to put God on that list! Acts 17:28 God first & U can't loose!

******

Happy New Year! Let this be a year of getting in alignment to the blessings of God. I am expecting great things from God this New Year!

******

If we could have as much passion and zeal for God as we do for the Super Bowl we could do great things for Him. Think about it.

******

Happy Easter to all. Remember we are joint heirs with Jesus. The same spirit that raised Christ from the dead dwells in me. Think about it.

eWitness

Karen Stone-Janiczek is available for speaking engagements and personal appearances. For more information contact:

Karen Stone-Janiczek
C/O Advantage Books
P.O. Box 160847
Altamonte Springs, Florida 32716

To purchase additional copies of this book or other books published by Advantage Books call our toll free order number at:
1-888-383-3110 (Book Orders Only)

or visit our bookstore website at:
www.advbookstore.com

Longwood, Florida, USA
"we bring dreams to life"™
www.advbooks.com

www.ingramcontent.com/pod-product-compliance
Lightning Source LLC
La Vergne TN
LVHW051130080426
835510LV00018B/2335